PICTURE
START

© 2001 Ron Mann
Text: Solomon Vesta
Still Crazy After All These Years: Marijuana Prohibition 1937-1997 by Keith Strube, Executive Director
NORML © 2001 NORMAL
What Dope Does to the Movies © 2001 Jonathan Rosenbaum
"Sing About a Reefer Five Feet Long": Marijuana in Popular Music © 2001 John P. Morgan, M.D.
Front cover by Paul Mavrides

All rights reserved. No part of this book may be reproduced or transmitted in any form, including photocopying, recording in any audio/visual format, or by any information storage and retrieval system without the written permission of the publisher.

We acknowledge the financial support of the Government of Canada through the Book Publishing Industry Development Program for our publishing activities.

ISBN (Canada): 1-894020-96-0
ISBN (United States): 1-57027-107-0

Published outside of Canada by **Autonomedia**
POB 568 Williamsburgh Station, Brooklyn, New York 11211-0568 USA
info@autonomedia.org
www.autonomedia.org

Published in Canada by **Warwick Publishing**
162 John Street, Toronto, ON M5V 2E5
www.warwickgp.com

Distributed in Canada by **General Distribution Services Ltd.**
325 Humber College Blvd., Toronto, ON M9W 7C3

Book design by Kimberley Young
Sonny Bono photo on page 73 courtesy AP/Wide World Photos

Printed in Canada

the PAGED experience

Marijuana, the dried leaves and flowers of the Indian hemp weed, is used in the form of a cigarette. Marijuana smoking, experts point out, can make a helpless addict of its victim within weeks causing physical and moral ruin and death. Should you ever be confronted with the temptation of taking that first puff of a marijuana cigarette, don't do it.

W
Warwick Publishing
Toronto
www.warwickgp.com

A
Autonomedia
New York
www.autonomedia.org

GRASS

GRASS

GRASS

GRASS

GRASS

GRASS

THE WAR ON DRUGS is not accurately named because I can go into any city and find hundreds of places to buy drugs legally... drugstores with large, neon signs touting their product. It would be more fair to call it a war on non-corporate drugs. We are a country of drug addicts, our children addicted to Prozac, Ritalin, and sugar — eventually cigarettes and alcohol.

This movie peels the mask off the war on marijuana, the primary victim of the drug war, and shows its historical significance. I am extremely proud to be a part of it.

–Woody Harrelson

The Official TRUTH
If you smoke it...
You Will Kill People

Although people around the world have been smoking marijuana for thousands of years, the custom only reached the United States at the beginning of the 20th century — when it arrived in the Southwest with a wave of Mexicans looking for work.

Laredo, Texas circa 1912

To these poor labourers, smoking marijuana was a way to relax after a long day of working in the fields. But white Americans along the border didn't much like these foreigners or their strange customs.

Marijuana, it was rumored, gave the Mexicans superhuman strength, and turned them into bloodthirsty murderers.

One evening in El Paso, some white Texans were allegedly attacked by a Mexican that "went crazy on the killer weed".

The El Paso Times

ALIEN WEED MAKES MAN INTO KILLER

El Paso Or...

Moving swiftly, the El Paso city council passed a law banning possession of marijuana. Supposedly designed to control marijuana, the law quickly became a way for the city to control *Mexicans*.

Unlike the people of El Paso, most Americans had never even *heard* of marijuana. They were more concerned about the rising addiction to opium, morphine, cocaine, and heroin — which were all serious public health issues.

But instead of treating drug addiction as a public health problem, the federal government put control of these drugs in the hands of the Treasury Department — who created the

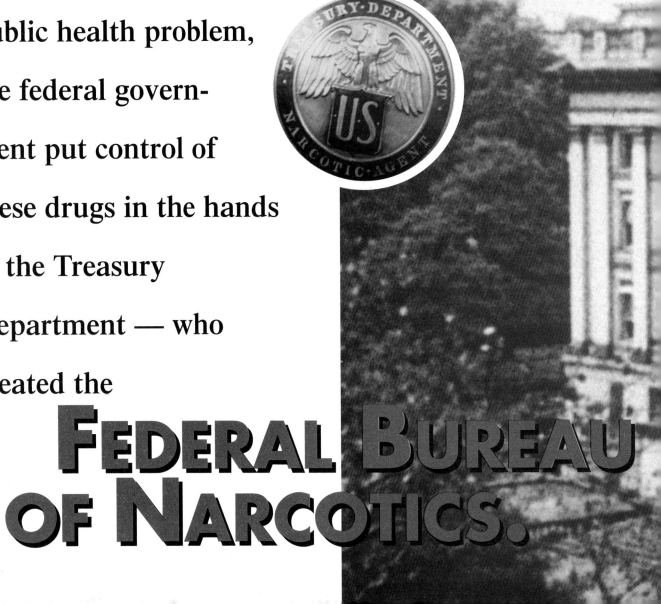

Treasury Department, Washington, D.C. circa 1930

FEDERAL BUREAU OF NARCOTICS.

America's first drug Czar was Harry J. Anslinger.

"The Treasury Department intends to pursue a relentless warfare against the despicable dope peddling vulture who preys on the weakness of his fellow man."

A "law and order" evangelist, Anslinger would shape America's attitude toward marijuana for generations to come.

Like many Americans, Anslinger was a prohibitionist.

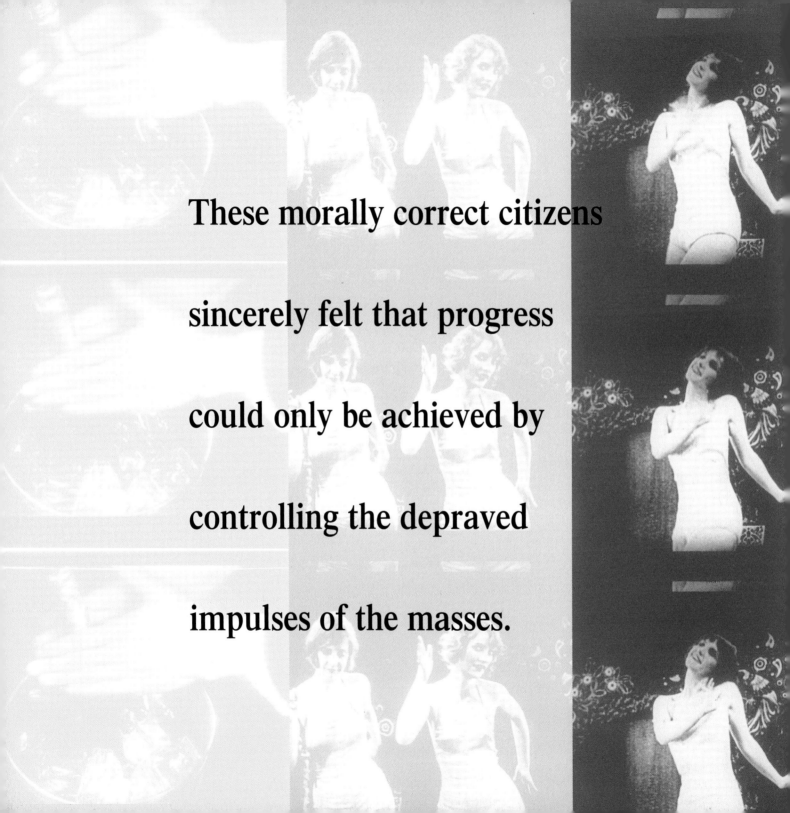

These morally correct citizens

sincerely felt that progress

could only be achieved by

controlling the depraved

impulses of the masses.

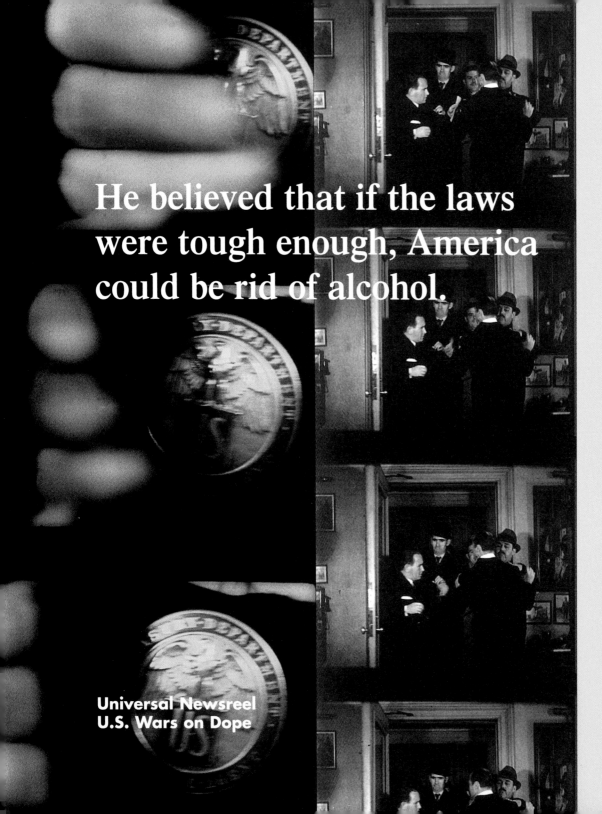

He believed that if the laws were tough enough, America could be rid of alcohol.

**Universal Newsreel
U.S. Wars on Dope**

Move over J. Edgar Hoover, here come the agents of the Federal Bureau of Narcotics.

Put enough people in jail, and eventually the public will learn to

behave...

And he applied this same philosophy to mounting the government's war on drugs.

Customs Agent
"You got any
merchandise
obtained in Canada
or abroad?"

Traveller
"No."

Customs Agent
"Have you any
liquor?"

Traveller
"No."

Customs Agent
"Get outta the
car. Let's take
a look at it."

WAR ON DOPE GETS RESULTS

Harry Anslinger Directs Nation's War On Drug Smuggling

A national drive was described as "the largest round up of big sellers and sources of supply of narcotics that has ever been undertaken in this country."

Harry J. Anslinger, U.S. Commissioner of Narcotics, inspects part of $7,000,000 seizure by Federal agents. The shoe, held by the commissioner, had secret compartment for narcotics.

Like J. Edgar Hoover, Anslinger posed for the cameras, creating the impression that he was smashing one major dope ring after another.

But he found out quickly that policing 48 states on a Depression-strapped budget was impossible.

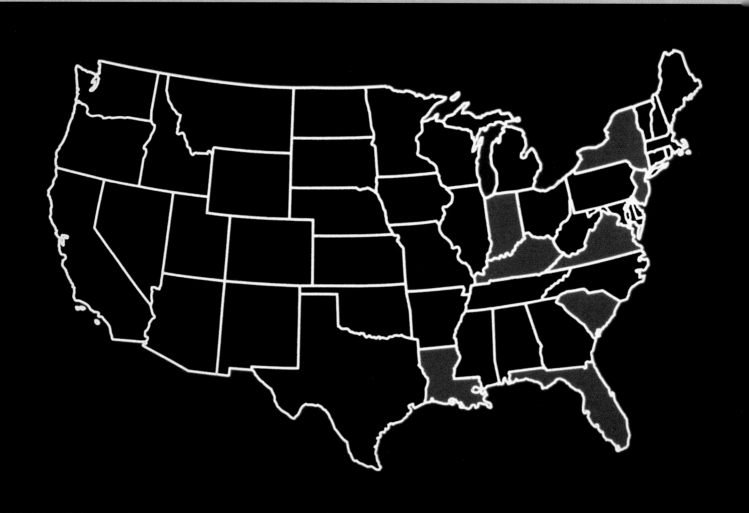

His solution was to try to convince the states to police <u>local</u> drug traffic themselves.

Campaigning tirelessly, he lobbied each state to sign a joint agreement to commit state resources to fighting drugs.

But only nine states signed on.

The other 38 viewed it as federal interference in their affairs. It was a major defeat for the young drug commissioner. But he wasn't the type to give up.

Meanwhile, marijuana, carried by West Indian sailors, arrived in port cities like New Orleans.

Known as "**muggles**", "**tea**", or "**reefer**",

Have you ever met that funny reefer man? Reefer man.

it was popular with the jazz crowd because it made music sound so good. From <u>here</u>, musicians carried it up the Mississippi to urban centers in the North.

Have you ever met that funny reefer man? Reefer man.

THE NEW OFFICIAL TRUTH

If you smoke it...

YOU WILL GO
INSANE

With marijuana showing up in the big cities, Anslinger realized it might be the answer to his problem. If he could persuade white America that marijuana was a deadly <u>menace</u>, frightened voters might push their state legislators to sign on to his Uniform Narcotics Act.

He is hopelessly and incurably insane.
A condition caused by the drug marijuana

Determined to get the Act passed, Anslinger unleashed a media campaign to make the public believe that this little-known plant growing at the side of rural roads, was the biggest threat America had ever faced.

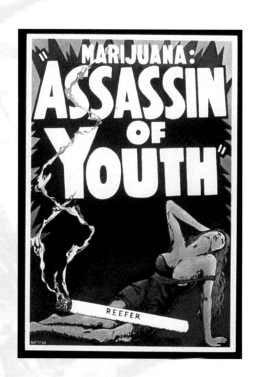

Parents beware! Your children, homeward bound from school, are being introduced to a new danger in the form of a drugged cigarette — MARIJUANA! Parents beware! Your children, homeward bound from school, are being introduced to a new danger in the form of a drugged cigarette — MARIJUANA! Parents beware! Your children, homeward bound from school, are being introduced to a new danger in the form of a drugged cigarette — MARIJUANA! Parents beware! Your children, homeward bound from school, are being introduced to a new danger in the form of a drugged cigarette — MARIJUANA! Parents beware! Your children, homeward bound from school, are being introduced to a new danger in the form of a drugged cigarette — MARIJUANA! — MARIJUANA! — MARIJUANA!

Harry J. Anslinger Radio Address *circa 1936*

Anslinger's campaign was tailor-made for the lurid tabloid press and, supported by an army of moralist groups, it captured the public's imagination.

America is threatened by a new drug menace! Street corner vendors whose stock-in-trade is the deadly loco-weed marijuana, pass it out in cigarette form. From ingeniously concealed containers, the reefers go to the waiting hands of deluded youngsters

The constant use of these marijuana cigarettes causes temporary insanity!

temporary insanity!
temporary insanity!
temporary insanity!
temporary insanity!

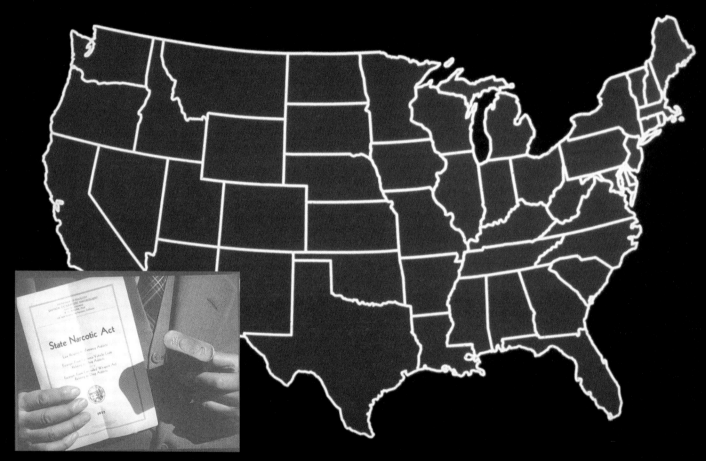

The propaganda campaign was successful
beyond Anslinger's wildest dreams. One by one,
state after state signed on…

But now, frightened out of their minds, the American public demanded that the federal government pass *new* laws to fight marijuana.

Terrified voters wanted action

— and their government responded.

Without any public debate, scientific inquiry, or political objection, the Marijuana Tax Act was signed into law by President Roosevelt.

June 14, 1937

The act prohibited possession of marijuana anywhere in the United States without a special tax stamp from the Treasury Department.

And the Treasury department didn't give <u>out</u> any stamps — effectively making marijuana illegal.

Overnight, a new class of criminals was created.

The first person to be convicted was Samuel R.

Caldwell, a fifty-eight-year-old Denver man.

Sentencing him to four years hard labor at

Leavenworth, Judge J. Foster Symes said: "I

consider marijuana the worst of all narcotics. Under

its influence, men become beasts. In the future

I will impose the heaviest penalities.

The government is going to enforce this new law to the letter."

New York's prohibition-fighting mayor, Fiorello La Guardia, was somewhat skeptical of the government's claims that marijuana was causing

murder, rape and the destruction of America's youth. Wanting to get the facts, he commissioned a study by a group of thirty-one impartial scientists.

Fiorello La Guardia, Mayor of New York

After six years of medical and sociological reserch, the La Guardia commission found:

- smoking marijuana did not lead to violent or anti-social behavior;

- smoking marijuana did not cause uncontrollable sexual urges;

- smoking marijuana did not alter a person's basic personality structure.

Item by item, the commission's report disproved every negative effect claimed by Harry Anslinger.

THE MARIJUANA PROBLEM IN THE CITY OF NEW YORK

by

Mayor LaGuardia's
Committee on Marihuana

Published under the auspices of The Library Publications Committee

The New York Academy of Medicine

Furious, Anslinger used his influence with the press to have the report discredited, and destroyed every copy he could get his hand on.

Then, by restricting the supply of <u>marijuana</u>, he put a stop to any further research.

Not taking any chances, Anslinger ordered his men to dig up dirt on anyone who **disagreed with him,**

GENE KRUPA IS ARRESTED

He Denies He Sent Boy to Get Marihuana Cigarettes

SAN FRANCISCO, Jan 20 (U.P.) —Gene Krupa, swing-band leader, pleaded innocent today to a charge that he contributed to the delinquency of a minor by sending a 17-year-old boy to his hotel room for marihuana cigarettes.

Judge Thomas J. Foley continued the case to Jan. 26 on a motion by the defense attorney, J. W. Ehrlich. Mr. Krupa was arrested last night by Federal narcotics agents after appearing at a local theatre.

In continuing the case, Judge Foley made public a statement, which the youth, John Pateakos, of Bedford, Mass., made to the narcotics agents.

The District Attorney's office said that Federal agents arrested Pateakos and found marihuana cigarettes in his possession. Pat said to the band leader at the theatre.

At the city prison

and going on the offensive, he targeted the entertainment industry — which he saw as a degenerate moral influence.

MITCHUM NABBED IN MARIJUANA RAID

by RUTH BRIGHAM
Staff Correspondent International News

HOLLYWOOD, Sept. 1 (INS) Movie Hero Robert Mitchum, Actress Lila Leeds and two other persons were arrested early today when narcotic agents broke up a marijuana smoking party.

The arrests climaxed nearly a year of intense investigation by authorities in the local movie capital.

Narcotics agents managed to gain entrance into Miss Leeds sumptuous Laurel Canyon home by first making friends with her three boxer dogs.

ENTERED BY RUSE

The officers said they peeked through windows at the reefer party for nearly two hours before finally scratching on a rear screen door, imitating a dog which wanted into the house.

A.M. Barr, one of the arresting officers, disclosed that Mitchum - a $3,000 a week screen star - had been under surveillance for

Not wanting any trouble with the government, the Hollywood studios agreed to give Anslinger personal control over all movie scripts that mentioned drugs. And movies he felt sent the wrong message were just banned.

Canadian Film Banned in U.S.

Narcotics Addicts 'Sick' in U.S.

OTTAWA, Feb. 9 — (C.P.) — The United States Government has temporarily banned the Canadian movies before circulation in the U.S.

Film Board production, 'de-addict as a sick man, but in the U.S., he is not considered a sick man but a criminal. Thus, after a private showing in New York, a request was forwarded that the film be revised before American distribution can be allowed.

Already in circulation in Can-

A CODE
TO GOVERN THE MAKING
OF MOTION PICTURES

the

Reasons Supporting It

and the

Resolution for Uniform

Interpretation

Motion Picture Association of America, Inc.

1946

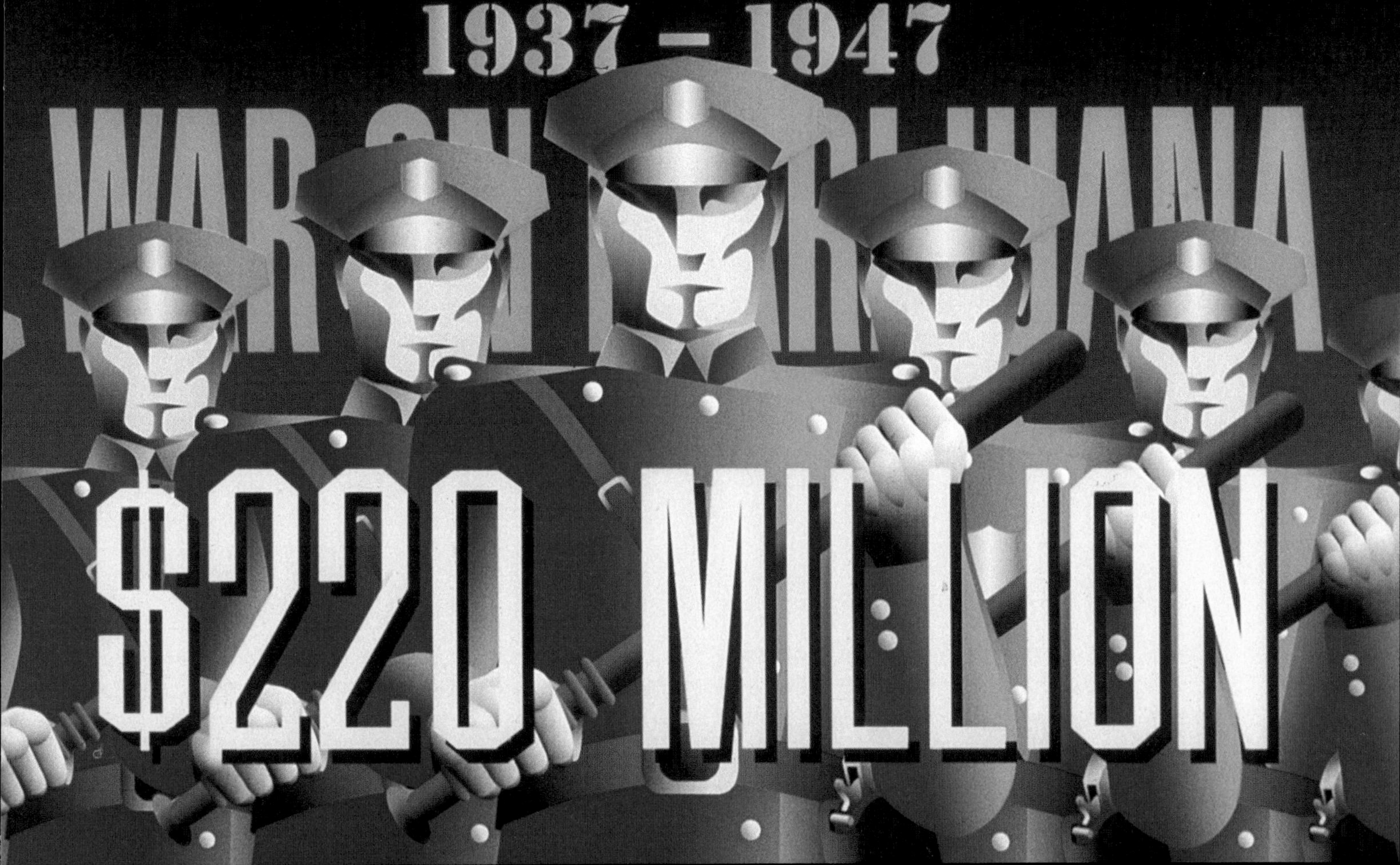
1937 – 1947
$220 MILLION

Official Replacement TRUTH
If you smoke it...
YOU WILL BECOME A
Heroin Addict!

By the early 1950s, concern about marijuana was overshadowed by a <u>new</u> media scare …

rising heroin addiction among teens who were drifting into crime to support their habit.

This heroin scare gave an aging Anslinger a new way to attack marijuana and respond to anyone who might doubt its terrible danger. Smoking marijuana, he declared, was a direct "stepping stone" to heroin addiction.

Remember—
Most "H" Users
Started
On Marijuana

An individual lad who tries the drug just for fun, or experiments with it, acts exactly like the person who loads the gun, puts the bullet in, puts it up to his head, very carefully hopes for the best and pulls the trigger.
"Tea, Horse and Crime" circa 1951

Interviewer:
May I have your name
please?
Robert Conlin:
Robert M. Conlin.
Commander of the
Detective Bureau, Culver
City Police department,
Culver City California.
Interviewer:
Is there any general per-
sonality traits that
would apply to addicts?
Robert Conlin:
Well, yes. Most of these
addicts are very sick and
they are a menace and
have to be arrested. I
get a lot of self satis-
faction from arresting
those people.
Interviewer:
And what about teenage
addiction? How does that
come about usually?
Robert Conlin:
They start out by using
marijuana.

 Appearing at the Kefauver crime hearings, Anslinger backed Senator Hale Bogg's proposal to increase penalties for all <u>drug</u> offenses. Tougher penalties were needed, he said, because behind every <u>narcotics</u> peddler, there was a Communist preparing to overthrow our government.

Senate Crime Hearings circa 1951

Even though there was absolutely no proof of a communist plot to dope up America, the country was in the grip of Cold War hysteria, and <u>no</u> politician could afford to look soft on communism.

DOPE

COMMUNIST CHINA'S ROLE IN THE INTERNATIONAL DRUG TRAFFIC

By HARRY J. ANSLINGER

Millions of dollars obtained through the sale of opium and other narcotics are used by the Communist regime of Mainland China for political purposes and to finance agents who have been found actively engaged in subversive activities.

Taking Anslinger's advice, President Truman signed the <u>Bogg's Act</u> — which dramatically increased penalties for possession, and ordered mandatory minimum sentences.

BOGGS ACT 1951
PASSED

On a roll, Anslinger agitated for even tougher laws… and got President Eisenhower to push them through Congress.

Narcotic Control Act
1956
PASSED

The Narcotic Control Act put marijuana in the same category as heroin — and made it subject to the same penalties. A first conviction for possession

was punished with a mandatory prison term of two to ten years. In addition, a number of states added their *own* penalties. In Missouri, a second conviction for possession could get you life.

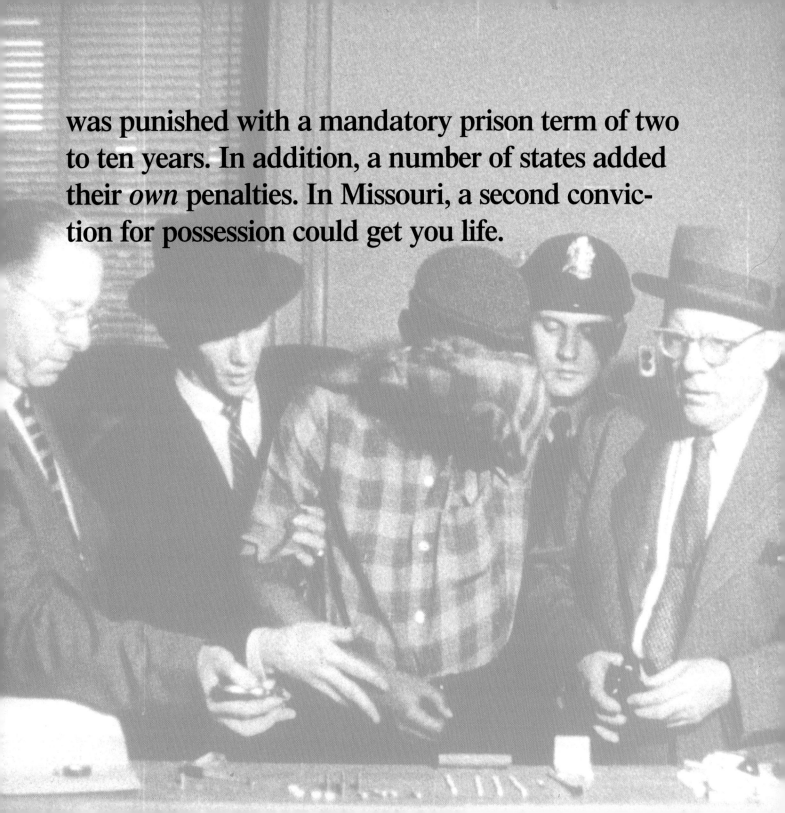

Setting his sights higher, Anslinger went to the

U.N. and used America's influence to persuade

over a <u>hundred</u> countries to consolidate their

various <u>drug</u> agreements into a <u>single</u>, inflexible

convention, outlawing marijuana around the world.

This was the ultimate achievement in Anslinger's

relentless crusade to criminalize marijuana use.

SINGLE CONVENTION ON NARCOTIC DRUGS 1961

To Harry Jacob Anslinger, Distinguished Citizen. In your dedicated efforts to combat the illegal traffic in narcotic drugs, you have fashioned an effective organization to pursue this objective. Your noteworthy achievements in this field have earned for you the respect of the world community.   Signed John F. Kennedy.

In leaving the bureau he'd built up under five different presidents, Anslinger warned his successors of an impending drug revolution, which he felt would be nothing less than an <u>assault</u> on the foundations of Western civilization.

Official TRUTH for a New Generation

IF YOU SMOKE IT...

You will WITHDRAW FROM REALITY

Lose All Motivation

UNDERMINE NATIONAL SECURITY

A responsibility only to one's self. Like liberty and the pursuit of pleasure. The new declaration of independence for the teenager around the world. Smoke a joint, burn a little grass. Pot parties. Roach parties. Main liners. Skin pop. Shoot some crystal. The language of the narcotic and marijuana user. The language of a large and ever increasing number of teenagers. Starting in high school on Benzedrine and Dexedrine pep pills it is not long before many soon graduate to marijuana. For some it quickens sexual desire, for some it is the release of sexual inhibitions. But whatever it is, teenagers are going for it. It may be the forerunner of a new drug society out of some science fiction writer's imagination. Will drugs pave the road to destruction for the now generation?

On campuses across the country, a whole new generation discovered <u>drugs</u>. Rebellious and willing to experiment, they found they liked altering their consciousness.

Allen Ginsberg poet

Jerry Garcia musician

Timothy Leary psychologist and author

Gradually, the perception that marijuana was dangerous began to change. Many students saw smoking grass as a rejection of establishment values — a way of declaring their independence.

Golden Gate Park Be-In, San Francisco 1967

The new head of the Federal Bureau of Narcotics, Henry Giordana, began to realize he had a problem.

To address it, he developed a campaign he hoped

Sonny Bono:
"If you become a pothead, you risk blowing the most important time

of your life, your teenage. That unrepeatable time for you to grow

would be believable to the younger generation…

up and to prepare for being an adult that can handle problems and

make something meaningful out of life. Or, you have the choice to

have the courage to see and deal with the world for what it real-

If you smoke marijuana, you will become an

ly is — Far, far from perfect but for you and for me the only one

there is."

unmotivated, dysfunctional, *loser*.

Because so many were trying marijuana without any ill effects, the public demanded to know more. And for the <u>first</u> time, the Federal government approved scientific testing.

Palo Alto Veterans Hospital, California circa 1967

Dr. Leo E. Hollister, Assoc. Chief of Staff

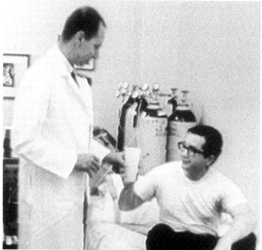

Dr. Leo E. Hollister
"The plain fact is none of us know very much about this drug in any
verifiable way."

"Well Bill, it's been about two hours since you got the drug, How do
you feel?"

Bill (the subject)
"Fantastic."
"Defiant? Not at all. Business like? Not at all. Friendly?
Extremely. This is ridiculous."

Nurse
"Would you be interested in taking part in a study like this again?"

Bill
"Oh!"

Nurse
"And having the same type of drug?"

Bill
"Sure!"

Nurse
"You would. It's been a very pleasant experience for you."

Bill
"I'll do it anytime you want."

Doctor
"We found out that the drug makes people happy. It makes them intoxicated and finally it makes them sleepy. Which is about what marijuana users were telling us happened all the time."

Whether the younger generation was presented as drugged-out hippies or anti-war protesters, conservative America reacted with a fear and hatred that threatened to pull the country apart. Manipulating the fears of what he termed the "Silent Majority", Richard Nixon built his campaign for the presidency around an emotion-ally-charged central issue — *restoring law and order*.... And it worked.

As President, Nixon was determined to be seen as the toughest crime-fighter ever. But *most* crimes fell under <u>State</u> jurisdiction, so Nixon wasn't allowed to get involved. However, there was one area where the federal goverment <u>did</u> have power — <u>drug</u> crime.

Early in his first term, Nixon launched Operation Intercept — a military-style exercise, officially described as "the country's largest peacetime search and seizure operation". In it, two thousand Customs agents were deployed along the Mexican border. Their orders... Stop the marijuana.

Although more than 5 million American and Mexican citizens passed <u>through</u> this dragnet, practically no marijuana was intercepted. After three weeks, Operation Intercept was abandoned.

Police Training Film *circa 1969*

In the day to day conduct of your police duties no matter how or for what reason you're called to investigate a situation in a residence, use your eyes to detect evidence of marijuana, hashish or narcotic violations.

There are some noticeable differences between a marijuana or "grass" joint and the butt of an ordinary cigarette, clearly visible even at a distance, to those who use their eyes. This is, of course, marijuana itself — the best evidence of all.

The evidence you're looking for is here alright, but it
has to be located before you can read it — use your
eyes. Ashtrays are logical places to use your eyes for
evidence of marijuana violations.

Now even *more* determined to appear tough
on crime, Nixon poured federal money into
equipping, training, and educating local police
forces across America.

It has distinctive characteristics:
learn them — use your eyes. It also
has a distinctive aroma so use your
nose as well as your eyes.

As arrests skyrocketed, the convictions were no longer limited to minorities. Now, most of the people serving time were white, middle-class American kids.

As middle-class parents began asking, "Why is my kid in jail?", more and more Americans began to feel that the problem was not marijuana, but marijuana *laws*.

Support for reform of marijuana laws seemed to come from everywhere. Even federal officials agreed that harsh penalties were not working.

When Don Crowe was convicted of selling marijuana to an undercover agent there seemed reason for hope. It was his first offense after all and the amount had been small, less than one ounce. But the jury saw its duty, sentence: 50 years in prison. For Crowe, 25 years old, newly returned from Vietnam, it was a bitter pill.

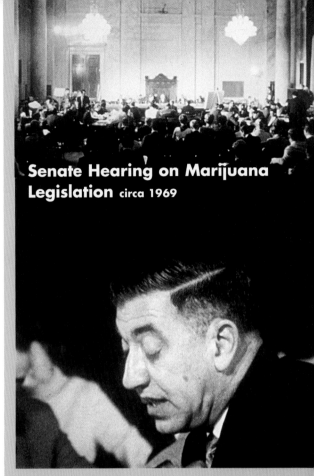

Senate Hearing on Marijuana Legislation circa 1969

Dr. Stanley Yolles
- Director, National Institute of Mental Health
"A conservative estimate of persons in the United States both juvenile and adult who have used marijuana at least once in the past is about 8 million and may go as high as 12 million. Can you imagine what would happen to the law enforcement and corrections system of this country if each of these 12 million people had been caught by a policeman when smoking his first marijuana cigarette? The first place in which legal reforms can be made is in the removal of mandatory minimum penalties in all cases of drug abuse."

Sensing the public's mood, Congress passed the Controlled Substances Act, which eliminated mandatory minimum sentences, and reduced penalties for possession.

OFFICIAL TRUTH FO

If you si

BAD T

WILL H

BUT WE DON'T KN

YOUR OWN GOOD

oke it...

HINGS

APPEN

W WHAT THEY ARE

Unwilling to let a bunch of effete liberals ruin his crime-fighting agenda, Nixon enlisted TV producers and show-business stars to send a strong moral message to "every home, every school and every church in America."

Repelled by the idea of softening *any* laws, Nixon maintained that until more was known about marijuana's dangers, the laws should not change. To this end, he made millions of dollars available to <u>find</u> those dangers.

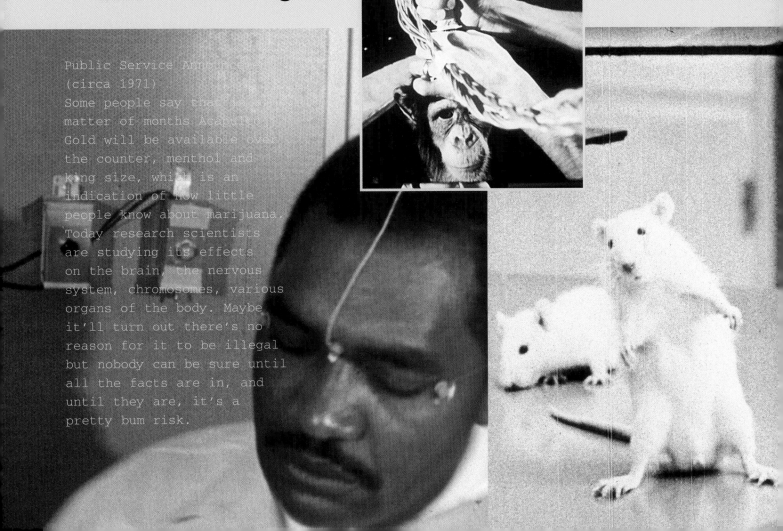

Public Service Announcement
(circa 1971)
Some people say that in a
matter of months Acapulco
Gold will be available over
the counter, menthol and
king size, which is an
indication of how little
people know about marijuana.
Today research scientists
are studying its effects
on the brain, the nervous
system, chromosomes, various
organs of the body. Maybe
it'll turn out there's no
reason for it to be illegal
but nobody can be sure until
all the facts are in, and
until they are, it's a
pretty bum risk.

The recommendations of the Commission in its

first report is that we do not feel that private

use or private possession in one's own home

should have the stigma of criminalization that

uh people who experiment should not be

criminalized for that particular behaviour.

Raymond P. Shafer, Chairman, National Commission on Marijuana and Drug Abuse

The Presidential Commission's Report on Marijuana found:

— marijuana use, in and of itself, did *not* cause crime;

— current laws against grass led to selective prosecution, and the police were suspected of <u>using</u> these laws to arrest people with objectionable hair styles, skin color, or politics;

— the enormous cost of trying to enforce laws against marijuana "overwhelmingly outweighed any deterrent value of these laws."

The Commission had conducted the most <u>comprehensive</u> and highly publicized <u>study</u> of marijuana ever done.

Furious, Nixon tossed it in a waste basket without ever reading it.

Doing the exact opposite of what was recommended, Nixon declared an all-out war on drugs.

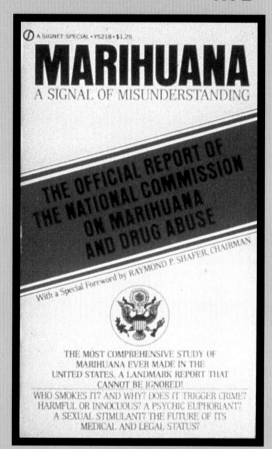

1972

His primary weapon:
the D.E.A. — a new
government agency
that combined all of
the goverment's
existing anti-drug
agencies into a single,
all-powerful
"super-agency".

Agent
"Last week we pulled 13 pounds of it up in about five different patches and we got another four o
five now that are really small patches but we're gonna go ahead and pull them up today."
Man with Microphone
"What do you do with it, you just come in and destroy the patch is that the idea?"
Agent
"We destroy the patch and we'll take it and just burn it."
Man with Microphone
"Apparently there is someone coming back here and cultivating it."
Agent
"Definitely, these are all in nice little neat rows and it's kind of a rotating crop they got some a
smaller than others."
Man with Microphone
"How good is Georgia pot?"
Agent
(laughing) I've never smoked it so I don't know."

Employing more than 4,000 analysts and agents, the DEA had the authority to request wiretaps, enter private homes <u>without knocking</u>, and gather intelligence on ordinary citizens.

Meanwhile, in suburbia, smoking pot had become the "in" thing for middle class adults — sort of like having a martini at happy hour.

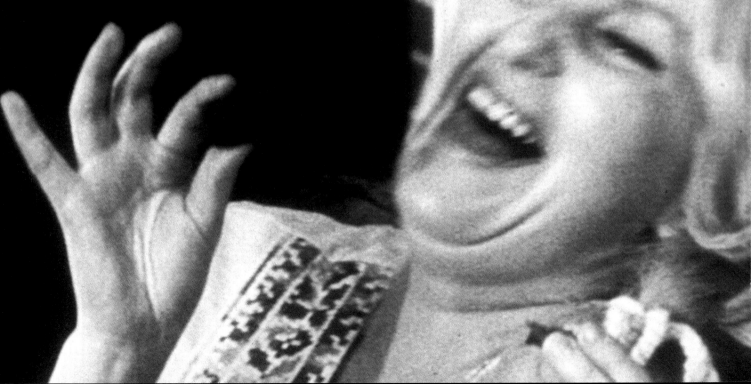

Betty Strand

Grandmother, age 56

"I've spent a lot of time with my daughter and her friends and they all smoke marijuana and so I had to try it."

Lawyer

"I first used pot back in the latter part of 1968 and have used it since then with some degree of regularity. I had some pot earlier today before I went down to court. I smoke at home, uh smoke at parties uh many places. To me its the question of the rights to life, liberty and the pursuit of happiness. You know, who owns me?!"

Keith Stroup Founder,
National Organization for the Reform
of Marijuana Laws

As smoking marijuana became increasingly mainstream, pro-pot activists began organizing support for decriminalization.

A political activist named John Sinclair became a symbol for the movement. He'd received a jail sentence of "10 for 2" — ten years in prison, for possession of two joints.

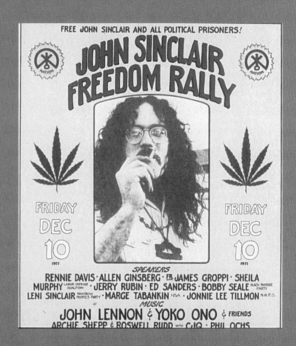

FREE JOHN SINCLAIR AND ALL POLITICAL PRISONERS!

JOHN SINCLAIR FREEDOM RALLY

FRIDAY DEC 10 1971

FRIDAY DEC 10 1971

SPEAKERS
RENNIE DAVIS · ALLEN GINSBERG · FB JAMES GROPPI · SHEILA MURPHY LABOR DEFENSE COALITION · JERRY RUBIN · ED SANDERS · BOBBY SEALE BLACK PANTHER PARTY
LENI SINCLAIR RAINBOW PEOPLES PARTY · MARGE TABANKIN NSA · JONNIE LEE TILLMON N.W.R.O.

MUSIC
JOHN LENNON & YOKO ONO & FRIENDS
ARCHIE SHEPP & ROSWELL RUDD with CJQ · PHIL OCHS

Keith
Stroup

"Last year in this country there were 226,000 marijuana related arrests and although the police sometimes tell us they are only interested in the pusher or the seller as they say, the fact is that only 7% of those arrests were against the seller. 93% of those arrests were for possession and use. Now what that means is there were about 200,000 young people in this country last year who were given an unnecessary criminal record and all that involves for the rest of their lives simply because they smoked grass something that is a relatively harmless thing to do. So, we're not trying to encourage the use of the drug in fact we're trying to discourage it, but we're trying to get the country to understand that there are other means to discourage the use of drugs other than the criminal law and in this case the use of the criminal law causes more harm than the drug itself."

Ann Arbor
City Ordinance
1972

Consistent with the changing times, the city of
Ann Arbor, Michigan passed an ordinance taking
marijuana possession *out* of the criminal code,
and making it a <u>minor</u> offense — the equivalent
of a parking ticket.

A year later, after a ground-breaking vote in its legislature, Oregon became the first state to completely decriminalize marijuana.

Tom McCall
Governor of Oregon

"Here is a state that is not afraid to found new ground in area where there is lot of hysteria."

"It's not gonna be very widely understood. But I think as you look back over the handling of drugs, if you can keep it in for a few years you'll see it was landmark legislation."

Decriminalization Bill
1973

PASSED

In 1974, with legal problems of his own, Richard Nixon resigned from the Presidency.

A study in Oregon, four years after decriminalization, showed no increase in marijuana use, and a substantial savings of tax dollars formerly spent on law enforcement.

By <u>that</u> time, ten other states had decriminalized marijuana.

Continuing Nixon's war on drugs, fill-in President Gerald Ford ordered U.S. forces to spray Mexican marijuana fields with the military defoliant paraquat.

But in the upcoming presidential elections, he 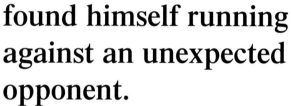 found himself running against an unexpected opponent.

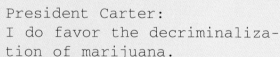

President Carter:
I do favor the decriminalization of marijuana.

I support a change in law,
in federal criminal penalties
for possession of up to one
ounce of marijuana. Leaving
the states free to adopt
whatever laws they wish con-
cerning marijuana.

Due in part to advocacy by the decriminalization movement, the government was finally preparing to abandon its war on marijuana-smokers.

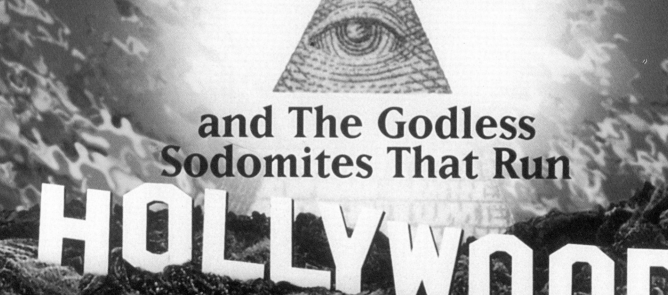

Fundamental Official Truth
If you smoke it...
YOU WILL BE IN THE GRIP OF
SATAN

and The Godless
Sodomites That Run
HOLLYWOOD

In the permissive 70's, marijuana seemed to be everywhere. Through movies and television, it had entered the popular culture…

But not everyone was laughing. Worried about teen-age marijuana use, a number of concerned parents organized pressure groups to fight the new drug culture.

In the midst of this backlash, Dr. Peter Bourne, Carter's chief drug policy advisor, was caught up in a scandal involving alleged cocaine use.

As the press had a field day, the President could no longer afford to appear <u>soft on drugs</u>. His proposal to decriminalize marijuana would <u>die in Congress</u>.

Whatever Happened

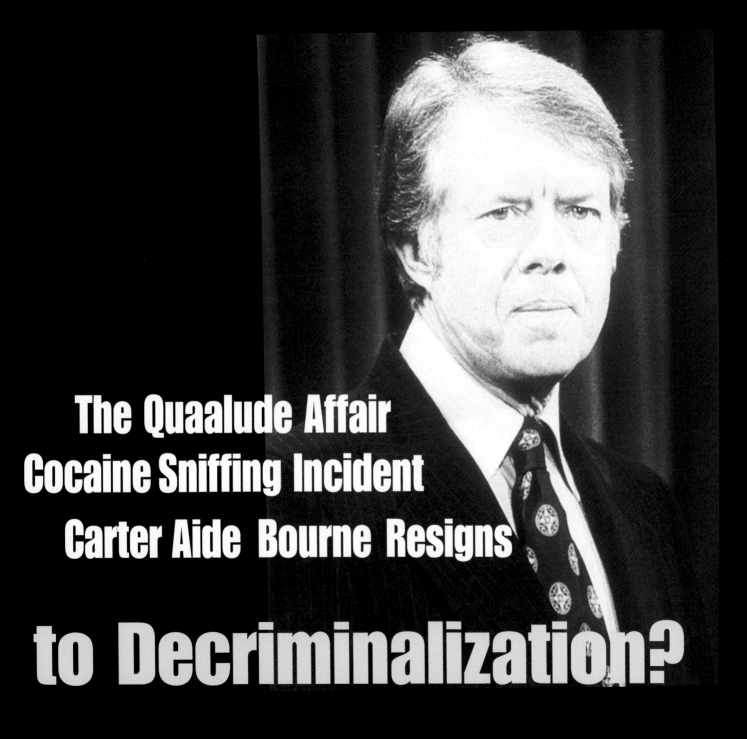

The Quaalude Affair
Cocaine Sniffing Incident
Carter Aide Bourne Resigns

to Decriminalization?

Driven by a sense of righteous indignation, the religious right mobilized into a potent political force.

VOTE

NOT FAIR TO THE NATURAL TRADITIONAL FAMILY

Reagan Presidential
Campaign 1980

"Leading medical
researchers are coming
to the conclusion that
marijuana, pot, grass
whatever you want to
call it, is probably
the most dangerous drug
in the United States and
we haven't begun to find
out the all of the ill
effects but they are
permanent ill effects.
The loss of memory for
example

After a brief period of tolerance, America was poised for a major swing the other way.

This is your brain on
drugs. Any questions?

Just say no.

no.   Just say no.   Just say no.   Just say no.

ANTI-DRUG ABUSE ACT 1986

... signed legislation allowing law enforcement agencies to seize cash and property from suspected drug offenders.

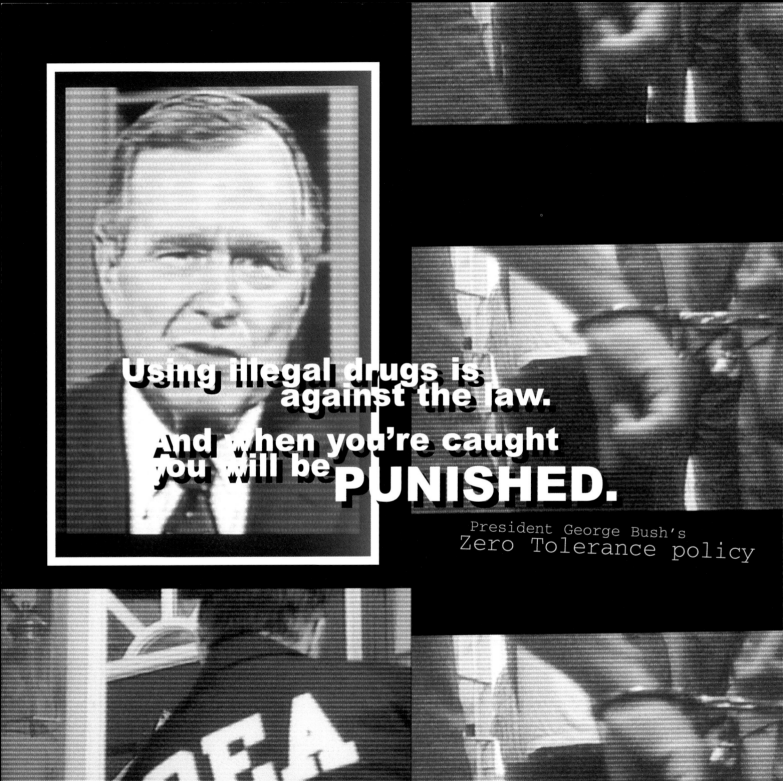

Using illegal drugs is against the law.
And when you're caught you will be **PUNISHED.**

President George Bush's
Zero Tolerance policy

Some think there won't be room for them in jail. WE'LL MAKE ROOM.

THE RULES HAVE CHANGED.

WAR ON MARIJUANA

1980 – 1998

$214.7 BILLION

NEW YORK CITY 1999

WHO AM I HURTING

DRUG WAR MEANS POLICE STATE INC.

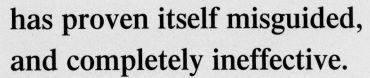

Since President Clinton took office, over three million people have been arrested for possession of marijuana — more than under any previous administration. The United States' government continues to wage a war on grass that time and time again, has proven itself misguided, and completely ineffective.

Fiorello La Guardia
That being so, the orderly thing to do under our form of government is to abolish a law which cannot be enforced, a law which the people of the country do not want enforced.

what dope does to movies
by Jonathan Rosenbaum

To the memory of Paul Schmidt

Consider how the camera cuts from Richie Havens's face, guitar, and upper torso during his second number in *Woodstock* (1970) to a widening vista of thousands of clapping spectators, then to a much less populated view of the back of the bandstand, where there's no clapping, watching, or listening — just a few figures milling about near the stage. What's going on? This radical shift in orientation and perspective — a sudden movement from total concentration to Zenlike disassociation — is immediately recognizable as part of being stoned, and Michael Wadleigh's epic concert film, which significantly has about the same duration as a marijuana high, is one of the first studio releases to incorporate this experience into its style and vision.

Or think of the way *Blade Runner* (1982) starts: a long, lingering aerial view of Los Angeles in the year 2019, punctuated by dragon-like spurts of noxious yellow flames, with enormous closeups of a blue eye whose iris reflects these sinister, muffled explosions. Or consider the zany, spastic contortions of Steve Martin en route to an elevator in *All of Me* (1984) — torn schizophrenically between his own identity and that of a recently reincarnated Lily Tomlin. Two hostile forces and divided wills twist his elastic, string-bean body into a wild succession of contradictory jazz riffs, a riddled battlefield careening this way and that under opposing orders.

Better yet, contemplate the hallucinatory special effects and the screwy changes of tone in Joe Dante movies like *Gremlins* (1984), *Matinee* (1993), or *Small Soldiers* (1998), the wide-angle distortions and fantasy premises of films like Bob Balaban's *Parents* (1989) and Raul Ruiz's *Three Lives and Only One Death* (1996), or the ambiguous netherworld between thoughts and realities comprising Stanley Kubrick's *Eyes Wide Shut* (1999).

All of these experiences have something to do with dope. None of them would look or sound or play the same way today if marijuana hadn't seized and transformed the style of pop movies thirty years ago. This isn't to say that the filmmakers in question are necessarily teaheads, or that the people in the audience have to be wigged-out in order to appreciate these efforts. Stoned consciousness by now is a historical fact, which means that the experiences of people high on grass have profoundly affected the aesthetics of movies for everyone: filmmakers and spectators, smokers and non-smokers alike.

It all started around the same time that movies as a whole got shaken up. Exploding Sixties culture opened up the way to all sorts of outside influences. From England came the Beatles and the Rolling Stones; from France came the New Wave movies of Godard, Resnais, Rivette, and Truffaut; political models were exported from China and Cuba, religious models from India and Japan. Meanwhile, the herbal emblems of certain American minorities — the peyote of Indians, the reefers of blacks — got tossed into the same heady stew, adding a congenial flavor to all the rest.

What did dope do to the movies, exactly? First of all, it changed the ways that people looked and listened. Then it altered the ways that they accepted what they saw and heard:

In Los Angeles, among the independent filmmakers at their midnight screenings

I was told that I belonged to the older generation, that Agee-alcohol generation they called it, who could not respond to the new films because I didn't take pot or LSD and so couldn't learn just to accept everything.

This is Pauline Kael, writing in 1964. The article in question is the introduction to her first collection of movie reviews, an essay which is significantly subtitled, "Are the Movies Going to Pieces?" Clearly alarmed at the gradual erosion of audience interest in coherent, well-turned narratives and the growing enthusiasm for jazzy innovations from abroad, Kael could already see a relation between this shift in taste and the widening popularity of grass over alcohol, a change that was generational as well as cultural. Appropriately enough, this revelation took place at a midnight movie — one of those dark, damp retreats of the Sixties where stoned consciousness first came into full bloom. As J. Hoberman and I explored at some length in the book *Midnight Movies*, marijuana and midnight screenings have nearly always been closely interconnected, if only because dope generally helps to foster a wider and more hedonistic spirit of aesthetic openness.

For many experimental filmmakers, the requirement placed on most films to tell a story often stands in the way of other possible pleasures that movies can impart. The tendency to savor individual moments which pot encourages, sometimes at the expense of the whole — a trend towards fragmented experience which TV has also promoted — made consistent and realistic storylines less obligatory than they had been in previous decades. The qualities of pure spectacle found in Stanley Kubrick's *2001: A Space Odyssey* (1968) and diverse psychedelic fruit salads such as Fellini's *Satyricon* and *Performance* (both 1970) were generally dismissed and disparaged by Kael and other members of her generation. But potheads passionately embraced these movies, caring more about what they had to show than what they had to say. Another older critic, Andrew Sarris, revised his negative opinion of *2001* somewhat after he returned to the film with the aid of a little herbal stimulation, and the fact that he could report on such an undertaking without embarrassment in the *Village Voice* is emblematic of the relative freedom and relaxation of that period.

With the advent of such purely visual masterpieces of the late Sixties as *2001*, *Point Blank*, and *Playtime*, movies were beginning to resemble such purely aural experiences as record albums by the Beatles and Frank Zappa over the same period. They were becoming environments to wander about and wallow in, not merely compulsive plots that you had to follow, and sustaining certain contradictions — two-tiered forms of thinking whereby the mind could drift off in opposite directions at once — was part of the fun they were offering.

Other older critics retracted their original harsh judgements of *Bonnie and Clyde* (1967) after the film went on to become a box office smash with the youth market. Now here was a movie that had a detailed storyline — but one that was subject to frequent and abrupt changes of tone, as in Godard's *Breathless* and Truffaut's *Shoot the Piano Player*, where slapstick comedy and nostalgic romance alternated with tragic bloodbath violence. Just as a doper's stoned rap might veer in mid-sentence from a consideration of life to a consideration of toenails, movies were getting redefined as an art of the present tense where theoretically anything could happen, regardless of whether or not everyone in the audience came along for the ride.

The same year that Kael first acknowledged the influence of dope on film taste, Susan Sontag published her "Notes on Camp," which bore witness to a closely related phenomenon — the ironic appreciation of sincere art that was outrageously overblown. Sontag's examples ranged all the way from *Shanghai Express* to *King Kong*, expressing new routes to pleasure that could bypass the usual barriers between high and low forms of art. And if camp taste probably owed as much to gay sensibility as the learned pleasures of pot owed to black culture, there was a way in which these two minority interests often worked hand in glove. Consider the lasting success of *Reefer Madness* as a midnight camp classic long after it was released in earnest in 1940; and by the same token — or toke — one should add that stoned amusement helped to pave the success of such deliberate camp efforts as *Female Trouble* and *Beyond the Valley of the Dolls*, not to mention other midnight staples including *The Rocky Horror Picture Show*, *Eraserhead*, and George Romero's "Dead" trilogy.

If Robert Altman's movies in the early Seventies — *M*A*S*H*, *Brewster McCloud*, *McCabe and Mrs. Miller*, *The Long Goodbye* — reveal the overall impact of dope on movie consciousness, representing a halfway house between the softer dope influence of the Sixties and the harder edge it would take on in the later Seventies — this is because they reflect so many of the stylistic changes reflected above, at the same time that they frequently allude to drugs in their plots. The use of overlapping dialogue and offbeat musical accompaniments (such as the Leonard Cohen songs in *McCabe*, the bird lectures in *McCloud*, and the multiple versions of the title tune in *The Long Goodbye*) created a dense weave that made each spectator hear and understand a slightly different movie — and, given that these were crowd-ed, widescreen features, see a different movie as well. These movies were all spaced-out experiences which presented both bright communal activities (from army pranks to patriotic rallies to frontier-town gossip to hash brownies) and lonely, deranged individuals who stood outside these mystiques and pursued dreamy head-trips of their own. As a spectator, one was invited to identify with both positions — hearing the local prattle about whorehouse owner McCabe (Warren Beatty) and his legendary prowess with a gun, and sharing the same character's tongue-tied awkwardness and experience. Drifting between these contradictory options, one navigated one's way through Altman's languid zooms and uncentered camera movements like a doper gliding through different trains of thought, comically stumbling (like many of the characters) through hallucinatory environments where nothing was ever the way one assumed it to be.

...I occasionally use marijuana in preference to alcohol, and have for several decades. I say occasionally and mean it quite literally; I have spent about as many hours high as I have in movie theaters — sometimes 3 hours a week, sometimes 12 or 20 or more, as at a film festival — with about the same degree of alteration of my normal awareness.
                                          –Allen Ginsberg, 1965

Let's say that early period [up through Pierrot le fou] was my hippie period. I was addicted to movies as the hippies are addicted to marijuana. I don't smoke marijuana, but I don't need to

because movies are the same to
me...[and] now I'm over this movie
marijuana magic thing.
                    –Jean-Luc Godard, 1969

In more ways than one, The Movie as Trip profoundly altered the social trappings and atmosphere of filmgoing as well as the more purely formal and aesthetic aspects of the experience. In contrast to the quintessentially communal experiences of movies like *Gone With the Wind*, *The Wizard of Oz*, and *Casablanca* — movies for and about communities — the no less emblematic *2001* of the Sixties and *Apocalypse Now* of the Seventies made each spectator the hero of a new kind of drama, which was staged inside someone's head. In some ways this environmental experience could be attributed to tapping the atmospheric possibilities of Dolby sound, but in other respects it might be regarded as a throwback to the German Expressionist movie tradition that characterized such silent classics as *The Cabinet of Dr. Caligari*, *Metropolis*, *Faust*, and *Sunrise*, and which subsequently became more Americanized and mainstreamed in certain Disney cartoon features like *Snow White and the Seven Dwarfs* and *Pinocchio* — not to mention Orson Welles's live-action *Citizen Kane*.

You might even say that travelling down the river in *Apocalypse Now* — a movie whose origins can be traced in part back to Welles's unfulfilled first Hollywood project preceding Kane, to adapt Joseph Conrad's "Heart of Darkness" in terms of the present, with the camera taking the role of Marlow — was a little bit like taking a ride in Disneyland and Disney World, remaining passive and mesmerized while a parade of marvels and surprises glided past you or were heard from surrounding speakers. Whatever was happening was happening to you, the spectator, first of all, the character of special agent Benjamin L. Willard (Martin Sheen) only secondarily, and the drugged-out ambience of the trip as a whole — derived in part from Michael Herr's remarkable evocations of pot-drenched Vietnam combat experiences in his book *Dispatches* — made the surreal fantasy element that much stronger. Alas, this made the meaning of the war in Vietnam for the Vietnamese even more remote from American experience than it already was; the "real" drama of *Apocalypse Now* had little to do with the suffering and struggle of the native population and everything to do with Francis Ford Coppola, the viewer's true surrogate, penetrating the "heart of darkness" like Conrad's Kurtz and Marlow.

Screened at midnight, marijuana-drenched movies might have been experienced communally, but in more mainstream venues one could argue that they tended by design to atrophy into more private trips. To a certain extent, subsequent blockbusters like the Star Wars and Indiana Jones trilogies reflected some of the same amusement-park tendencies, because by this time video games and home viewing were beginning to replace theatrical screenings as the main form of movie experience.

This transition had something to do with dope, but was affected still more by the implicit social philosophies of the respective periods, which also helped to determine how dope was smoked. What began in the Sixties as an almost tribally shared collective pastime — being stoned at the movies — passed through the Me Generation of the late Seventies to become a more private and individualized experience in the Eighties and early Nineties. Seeing a movie like the recently revived *Yellow Submarine* — a feature-length cartoon set to Beatles songs — back in 1968, in any large U.S. theaters that tolerated toking in its theaters (and there were plenty of those back then), you virtually had a guarantee of getting at least a buzz whether you brought along joints or not. The air would be so thick with smoke that you could walk through sample whiffs of various grades on the way to your seat, getting slightly glazed in the process. Because it was more fashionable back then to share smoke with strangers, roaches were more prone to be passed down the aisles, creating a kind of spider's web of complicity between the different people in the audience, as well as between them and the events on screen.

As grass-smoking gradually returned to the living room, bedroom, and bathroom, where it first took hold in the Sixties before the pastime became public, this return to relative privacy — a high to be shared with friends, but not with strangers — was reflected in the more insular and insulated pop movies that came out. Compare *2010* to *2001*, *The Cotton Club* to *Singin' in the Rain*, *Dune* to *Forbidden Planet*, *Gimme Shelter* to *Woodstock*: in each case the social context becomes narrower while the individual head-trip looms larger. Taking the movie home with you on video or DVD not only keeps you off the streets; it also leaves the movie untested as a site for social interaction, hence less amenable to certain collective experiences — unless one finds a way of making it more interactive again.

Perhaps only with the current global interconnections of the internet and email are we beginning to return to comparable kinds of complicity in relation to movies — the renewed notion of a tribal community, reconfigured this time not in terms of viewing movies but in terms of discussing them and related subjects (and sometimes in terms of finding and swapping certain movies on video). Interestingly enough, this may also be affecting movie content: the fantasy-driven contradictions that dope-enhanced and dope-influenced movies used to embrace are making a welcome comeback, only this time they could just as well be labelled cybernetic as psychedelic in impulse — and the influence of musical sampling could be equally important. Who says that Forest Whitaker can't play a New Jersey samurai operating according to ancient warrior codes and working for the Mafia, in Jim Jarmusch's *Ghost Dog*? Twenty years ago the conceit would have been labeled a doper's reverie; today it still can be read that way, but it also sounds like a fantasy hatched on the internet.

(An early version of this article appeared in High Times, *March 1985; revised and updated, March 2000.)*

still crazy after all these years

MARIJUANA PROHIBITION 1937-1997

Report prepared by the National Organization for the Reform of Marijuana Laws (NORML) on the occasion of the 60th anniversary of the adoption of the "Marihuana Tax Act of 1937," August 2, 1997

Marijuana cultivation in the United States can trace its lineage some 400 years. Cultivation of marijuana for fiber continued in American through the turn of the 20th century. Marijuana first earned recognition as an intoxicant in the 1920s and 1930s. During this time, exaggerated accounts of violent crimes allegedly committed by immigrants intoxicated by marijuana became popularized by tabloid newspapers and the newly formed Federal Bureau of Narcotics. Congress approved the "Marihuana Tax Act of 1937" based almost entirely on this propaganda and misinformation.

Marijuana remains the third most popular recreational drug of choice in the United States despite 60 years of criminal prohibition. According to government figures, nearly 70 million Americans have smoked marijuana at some time in their lives. Of these, 18 million have smoked marijuana within the last year, and ten million are regular marijuana smokers. The vast majority of these individuals are otherwise law-abiding citizens who work hard, raise families, and contribute to their communities. They are not part of the crime problem and should not be treated as criminals.

The Clinton administration is waging a more intensive war on marijuana smokers than any other presidency in history. Presently, law enforcement arrests a marijuana smoker every 54 seconds in America at a tremendous cost to society. This represents a 60 percent increase in marijuana arrests since Clinton took office. Over ten million Americans have been arrested on marijuana charges since the National Commission on Marijuana and Drug Abuse issued its recommendation to Congress in 1972 to decriminalize marijuana.

Because of harsh federal and state penalties, marijuana offenders today may be sentenced to lengthy jail terms. Even those who avoid incarceration are subject to an array of additional punishments, including loss of driver's license (even where the offense is not driving-related), loss of occupational license, loss of child custody, loss of federal benefits, and removal from public housing. Under state and federal forfeiture laws, many suspected marijuana offenders lose their cars, cash, boats, land, business equipment, and houses. Eighty percent of the individuals whose assets are seized are never charged with a crime. Marijuana prohibition disproportionately impacts minorities.

Blacks and Hispanics are over-represented both in the numbers of arrests and in the numbers of marijuana offenders incarcerated. Blacks and Hispanics make up 20 percent of the marijuana smokers in the United States, but comprise 58 percent of the marijuana offenders sentenced under federal law last year.

Nonviolent marijuana offenders often receive longer prison sentences than those allotted to violent offenders. Most Americans do not want to spend scarce public funds incarcerating nonviolent marijuana offenders, at a cost of $23,000 per year. Politicians must reconsider our country's priorities and attach more importance to combating violent crime than targeting marijuana smokers.

Marijuana prohibition costs taxpayers at least $7.5 billion annually. This is an enormous waste of scarce federal dollars that should be used to target violent crime.

Marijuana prohibition makes no exception for the medical use of marijuana. The tens of thousands of seriously ill Americans who presently use marijuana as a therapeutic agent to alleviate symptoms of cancer, AIDS, glaucoma, or multiple sclerosis risk arrest and jail to obtain and use their medication. Between 1978 and 1996, 34 states passed laws recognizing marijuana's therapeutic value. Most recently, voters in two states — Arizona and California — passed laws allowing for the medical use of marijuana under a physician's supervision. Yet, states are severely limited in their ability to implement their medical use laws because of the federal prohibition of marijuana.

America tried alcohol prohibition between 1919 and 1931, but discovered that the crime and violence associated with prohibition was more damaging than the evil sought to be prohibited. With tobacco, America has learned over the last decade that education is the most effective way to discourage use. Yet, America fails to apply these lessons to marijuana policy. Stubbornly defining all marijuana smoking as criminal, including that which involves adults smoking in the privacy of their own homes, we are wasting police and prosecutorial resources, clogging courts, filling costly and scarce jail and prison space, and needlessly wrecking the lives and careers of genuinely good citizens.

Marijuana Use in America Before 1937: Sowing the Seeds for Prohibition

Marijuana cultivation in the United States can trace its lineage some 400 years. For most of our nation's history, farmers grew marijuana — then known exclusively as hemp — for its fiber content. Colonialists planted the first American hemp crop in 1611 near Jamestown, Virginia. Soon after, King James I of Britain ordered settlers to engage in wide scale farming of the plant.[1] Most of the sails and ropes on colonial ships were made from hemp as were many of the colonists' bibles, clothing, and maps.[2]

According to some historians, George Washington and Thomas Jefferson cultivated marijuana and advocated a hemp-based economy.[3] Some colonies even made hemp cultivation compulsory and called its production necessary for the "wealth and protection of the country."[4]

Marijuana cultivation continued as an agricultural staple in America through the turn of the 20th century. Marijuana first earned recognition as an intoxicant in the 1920s and 1930s. Recreational use of the drug became associated primarily with Mexican-American immigrant workers and the African-American jazz musician community. It was during this time that hemp was renamed "marihuana" and the plant's long-standing history as a cash crop was replaced with a new image: "The Devil's Weed."

In 1930, the federal government founded the Federal Bureau of Narcotics (FBN), headed by Commissioner Harry Anslinger. The group launched a misinformation campaign against the drug and enrolled the services of Hollywood and several tabloid newspapers. Headlines across the nation began publicizing alleged reports of insanity and violence induced by "reefer-smoking." Exaggerated accounts of violent crimes committed by immigrants reportedly intoxicated by marijuana became popularized. Once under the influence of the drug, criminals purportedly knew no fear and lost all inhibitions. For example, a news bulletin issued by the FBN in the mid-1930s purported that a user of marijuana "becomes a fiend with savage or 'cave man' tendencies. His sex desires are aroused and some of the most horrible crimes result. He hears light and sees sound. To get away from it, he suddenly becomes violent and may kill."[5]

Similar reports swept the country. A widely publicized issue of the *Journal of Criminal Law and Criminology* asserted that the marijuana user is capable of "great feats of strength and endurance, during which no fatigue is felt.... Sexual desires are stimulated and may lead to unnatural acts, such as indecent exposure and rape.... [Use of marijuana] ends in the destruction of brain tissues and nerve centers, and does irreparable damage. If continued, the inevitable result is insanity, which those familiar with it describe as absolutely incurable, and, without exception ending in death."[6]

A *Washington Times* editorial published shortly before Congress held its first hearing on the issue argued: "The fatal marihuana cigarette must be recognized as a deadly drug and American children must be protected against it."[7]

This steady stream of propaganda influenced 27 states to pass laws against marijuana in the years leading up to federal prohibition and set the stage both culturally and politically for the passage of the "Marihuana Tax Act in 1937." Rep. Robert L. Doughton of North Carolina introduced the Act in Congress on April 14, 1937, to criminalize the recreational use of marijuana through prohibitive taxation. The bill was the brainchild of Commissioner Anslinger who later testified before Congress in support of the bill. Congress held only two hearings to debate the merits of marijuana prohibition. The hearings totaled just one hour.[8]

Federal witness Harry Anslinger testified before the House Ways and Means Committee that "this drug is entirely the monster-Hyde, the harmful effect of which cannot be measured." He was joined by Assistant General Counsel for the Department of the Treasury, Clinton Hester, who affirmed that the drug's eventual effect on the user "is deadly." These statements summarized the federal government's official position and served as the initial justification for criminalizing marijuana smoking.[9]

The American Medical Association (AMA) represented the lone voice against marijuana prohibition before Congress. AMA Legislative Counsel Dr. William C. Woodward testified, "There is no evidence" that marijuana is a dangerous drug. Woodward challenged the propriety of passing legislation based only on newspaper accounts and questioned why no data from the Bureau of Prisons or the Children's Bureau supported the FBN's position. He further argued that the legislation would severely compromise a physician's ability to utilize marijuana's therapeutic potential. Surprisingly, the committee took little interest in Woodward's testimony and told the physician, "If you want to advise us on legislation, you ought to come here with some constructive proposals ... rather than trying to throw obstacles in the way of something that the federal government is trying to do."[10]

After just one hearing, the Ways and Means Committee approved the "Marihuana Tax Act." The House of Representatives followed suit on August 20 after engaging in only *90 seconds* of debate. During this abbreviated floor "discussion," only two questions were asked. First, a member of Congress from upstate New York asked Speaker Sam Rayburn to summarize the purpose of the bill. Rayburn replied, "I don't know. It has something to do with a thing called marijuana. I think it is a narcotic of some kind." The same representative then asked, "Mr. Speaker, does the American Medical Association support the bill?" Falsely, a member of the Ways and Means Committee replied, "Their Doctor Wharton (sic) gave this measure his full support ... [as well as] the approval [of] the American Medical Association."[11] Following this brief exchange of inaccurate information, the House approved the federal prohibition of marijuana without a recorded vote.

Doughton's bill sailed though the Senate with the same ease. The Senate held one brief hearing on the bill before overwhelmingly approving the measure. President Franklin Roosevelt promptly signed the legislation into law on August 2, 1937. The "Marihuana Tax Act" took effect on October 1, 1937. Thus began the criminal prohibition of marijuana that remains in place today.

Marijuana Prohibition Is a Failure: Millions of Americans Smoke Marijuana Despite Laws Outlawing Its Use

Marijuana remains the third most popular recreational drug of choice in the United States despite 60 years of criminal prohibition. Only alcohol and tobacco are regularly consumed by a greater percentage of the population. Clearly, prohibition fails to eliminate or even significantly deter the use of marijuana among the American public.

It is time to put to rest the myth that smoking marijuana is a fringe or deviant activity engaged in only by those on the margins of American society. In reality, marijuana smoking is extremely common and marijuana is the recreational drug of choice for millions of mainstream, middle class Americans. According to the most recent data from the United States Department of Health and Human Services (HHS), *nearly 70 million Americans have smoked marijuana at some time in their lives.*[12] Of these, 18 million have smoked within the past year, and approximately 10 million are current smokers (defined as having smoked at least once in the last month.)[13] In fact, HHS found that 57 percent of all current illicit drug users report that marijuana is the *only* illegal drug they have used; this figure rises to 77 percent if hashish (a more concentrated form of marijuana) is included.[14]

A recent national survey of voters conducted by the American Civil Liberties Union (ACLU) found that 34 percent — one third of the voting adults in the country — acknowledged having smoked marijuana at some point in their lives.[15] Many successful business and professional leaders, including many state and federal elected officials from both political parties, admit they used marijuana. It is time to reflect that reality in our state and federal legislation, and stop acting as if marijuana smokers are part of the crime problem. They are not, and it is absurd to continue spending limited law enforcement resources arresting them.

Marijuana smokers in this country are no different from their non-smoking peers, except for their marijuana use. Like most Americans, they are responsible citizens who work hard, raise families, contribute to their communities, and want to live in safe, crime-free neighborhoods. They are otherwise law-abiding citizens who live in fear of arrest and imprisonment solely because they choose to smoke marijuana for relaxation instead of drinking alcohol.

Marijuana prohibition is a misapplication of the criminal sanction which undermines respect for the law in general and extends government into inappropriate areas of private lives. Millions of Americans use marijuana; few abuse it. The government should limit its involvement in this issue solely to address and sanction irresponsible marijuana use. Responsible marijuana use causes no harm to society and should be of no interest to the federal government.

Law Enforcement Arrests a Marijuana Smoker Every 54 Seconds in America at a Tremendous Cost to Society.

In 1972, a blue-ribbon panel of experts appointed by President Richard Nixon and led by former Pennsylvania Governor Raymond Shafer concluded that marijuana prohibition posed significantly greater harm to the user than the use of marijuana itself. The National Commission on Marijuana and Drug Abuse recommended that state and federal laws be changed to remove criminal penalties for possession of marihuana for personal use and for the casual distribution of small amounts of marijuana.[16] That year, law enforcement arrested almost 300,000 Americans on marijuana charges.[17]

A 1982 National Academy of Sciences (NAS) report on marijuana reaffirmed that criminal justice approaches were inappropriate and harmful. It recommended not only that marijuana possession be decriminalized, but that lawmakers give serious consideration to creating a system of regulated distribution and sale.[18] Law enforcement arrested over 450,000 Americans for violating marijuana laws that year.[19]

In May of this year, research findings from a comprehensive, long term study performed by Kaiser Permanente concluded that no link existed between regular marijuana smoking and mortality and emphasized that marijuana prohibition posed the only significant health hazard to the user. The report advocated that "medical guidelines regarding [marijuana's] prudent use ... be established, akin to the common-sense guidelines that apply to alcohol use."[20] In 1995, the most recent year for which the federal government has arrest statistics, law enforcement charged almost 600,000 Americans with marijuana violations.[21] This figure is the greatest number ever recorded since marijuana prohibition began; it means that *one marijuana smoker is arrested every 54 seconds in America.*

Despite criticism that President Clinton is "soft" on drugs, annual data from the Federal Bureau of Investigation's (FBI) Uniform Crime Report demonstrate that Clinton administration officials are waging a more intensive war on marijuana smokers than any other presidency in history. Law enforcement arrested approximately 1.5 million Americans on marijuana charges during the first three years of Clinton's administration — 84 percent of them for simple possession. The average number of yearly marijuana arrests under Clinton (483,548) is 30 percent higher than under the Bush administration (338,998), and last year's total alone is more than double the 1991 total (287,850).[22]

Marijuana penalties vary nationwide, but most levy a heavy financial and social impact for the hundreds of thousands of Americans who are arrested each year. In 42 states, possession of any amount of marijuana is punishable by incarceration and/or a significant fine.[23] For example, individuals arrested for simple marijuana possession in Arizona may face eighteen months in jail and a $150,000 fine.[24] Many states also have laws automatically suspending the drivers' license of an individual if they are convicted of any marijuana offense, even if the offense was not driving related.

Penalties for marijuana cultivation and/or sale also vary from state to state. Ten states have maximum sentences of five years or less and eleven states have a maximum penalty of thirty years or more.[25] Some states punish those who cultivate marijuana solely for personal use as severely as large-scale traffickers. For instance, medical marijuana user William Foster of Oklahoma was sentenced to 93 years in jail in January 1997 for growing 10 medium-sized marijuana plants and 56 clones (cuttings from another plant planted in soil) in a 25-square-foot underground shelter.[26] Foster maintains that he grew marijuana to alleviate the pain of rheumatoid arthritis. Unfortunately, Foster's plight is not an isolated event; marijuana laws in six states permit marijuana importers and traffickers to be sentenced to life in jail.[27]

Even those who avoid state incarceration are subject to an array of punishments that may include submitting to random drug tests, probation, paying for mandatory drug counseling, loss of an occupational license, expensive legal fees, lost wages due to absence from work, loss of child custody, loss of federal benefits, and removal from public housing. In some states, police will notify the employers of people who are arrested. As a result, employees may lose their job.[28]

Federal laws prohibiting marijuana are also severe. Under federal law, possessing one marijuana cigarette or less is punishable by a fine of up to $10,000 and one year in prison, the same penalty as for possessing small amounts of heroin and cocaine. In one extreme case, attorney Edward Czuprynski of Michigan served 14 months in federal prison for possession of 1.6 grams of marijuana before a panel of federal appellate judges reviewed his case and demanded his immediate release.[29] Cultivation of 100 marijuana plants or more carries a mandatory prison term of five years. Large-scale marijuana cultivators and traffickers may be sentenced to death.

Presently, Congress is proposing that the amount of marijuana necessary to trigger the death penalty be substantially lowered. The "Drug Importer Death Penalty Act of 1997," introduced by admitted former marijuana smoker Newt Gingrich (R-GA.), would potentially sentence first offenders convicted of bringing more than 50 grams (less than two ounces) of marijuana across U.S. borders to life in prison without parole. Those offenders convicted for a second time — presumably the first offense would have been convicted before H.R. 41's enactment — would be sentenced to death. Thirty-seven members of Congress are present cosponsors of this bill.

Federal laws also deny entitlements to marijuana smokers. Under legislation introduced by Sen. Phil Gramm (R-Texas) and signed into law last year, states may deny cash aid (e.g., welfare, etc.) and food stamps to anyone convicted of felony drug charges. For marijuana smokers, this includes most convictions for cultivation and sale, even for small amounts and nonprofit transfers. Currently, a murderer, rapist, or robber could receive federal funds and benefits, but not most individuals convicted of cultivating a small amount of marijuana.

In addition, under both state and federal law, mere investigation for a marijuana offense can result in the forfeiture of property, including cash, cars, boats, land, business equipment, and houses. Amazingly, the owner does not have to be found guilty or even formally charged with any crime for the seizure to occur. In 1993, Illinois Congressman Henry Hyde (R) reported that 80 percent of the individuals whose assets are seized by the federal government under drug forfeiture laws are never charged with a crime.

Law enforcement often targets suspected marijuana offenders for the purpose of seizing their property, sometimes with tragic results. For example, millionaire rancher Donald Scott was shot and killed by law enforcement officials in 1992 at his Malibu estate in a botched raid. Law enforcement failed to find any marijuana plants growing on his property and later conceded that their primary motivation for investigating Scott was to eventually seize his land.[30]

State and federal marijuana laws also have a disparate racial impact on ethnic minorities. While blacks and Hispanics make up only 20 percent of the marijuana smokers in the U.S.,[31] they comprised 58 percent of the marijuana offenders sentenced under federal law in 1995.[32] State arrest and incarceration rates paint a similar portrait. For example, in Illinois, 57 percent of those sent to prison for marijuana in 1995 were black or Hispanic.[33] In California, 49 percent of those arrested for marijuana offenses in 1994 were black or Hispanic.[34] And in New York state, 71 percent of those arrested for misdemeanor marijuana charges in 1995 were non-white.[35]

Since the Shafer Commission reported their findings to Congress in 1972 advocating marijuana decriminalization, *over ten million Americans have been arrested on marijuana charges.* Marijuana prohibition is a failed public policy that is out of touch with today's social reality and inflicts devastating harm on millions of citizens.

Nonviolent Marijuana Offenders Often Serve Longer Sentences Than Murderers or Rapists.

Elected officials at both the state and federal level often engage in what the National Criminal Justice Commission calls "bait and switch." Employers of this technique exploit the public's natural fear of violent crime and propose harsh, sometimes mandatory anti-drug legislation in response. Unfortunately, this legislation seldom targets violent criminals or large drug traffickers. Rather, it often inflicts a devastating impact on minor, non-violent drug offenders.

For example, harsh federal and state sentences often apply to "all" marijuana distribution and "possession with the intent to distribute" offenses, regardless of whether any violence was associated with the event or the defendant is a significant marijuana trafficker. Even minor offenses may qualify for harsh mandatory sentences. This is a needlessly destructive policy that is both a misuse of the criminal process and a waste of criminal justice resources.

If combating violent crime is the reason for imposing harsh and unyielding mandatory sentences, then such legislation should solely target violent offenders. There is no justification for treating non-violent marijuana offenses differently, yet many laws continue to do so.

For instance, many adult marijuana smokers share marijuana on a nonprofit basis with friends. Under many state laws, this activity could subject them to lengthy prison sentences. Similarly, many seriously ill people — including AIDS and cancer patients — use marijuana to relieve their pain and suffering. Often their illness requires that a primary caregiver obtain marijuana for them. Many of these caregivers could serve a mandatory prison sentence if convicted under existing marijuana laws.

Also at great risk are the proprietors of cannabis buyers' clubs (CBCs) who supply marijuana to seriously ill patients who possess a doctor's recommendation. Despite operating with the tacit acceptance of local law enforcement, all clubs operate in violation of federal law and most are in violation of state law. Owners of these clubs, who sometimes grow medical marijuana on site, often face federal mandatory minimum sentences for their activities. For example, federal agents confiscated over 300 marijuana plants at a California CBC called Flower Therapy on April 24, 1997.[36] Even though the club operated in accordance with state law and the plants confiscated were grown for medicinal purposes only, the owners of the club face a mandatory minimum sentence of at least five years in prison if they are found guilty of cultivation. This mandatory sentence is equal to the average prison time served by defendants convicted of violent crimes like manslaughter and is over one year longer than the average federal sentence served for assault.[37] Likewise, individual patients preferring to avoid the black market altogether and grow a few marijuana plants in their homes are also subject to stiff state and/or federal penalties.

Marijuana possession and cultivation offenses have absolutely nothing to do with violence, yet people convicted of these offenses regularly serve longer sentences than those convicted of violent offenses, including rape and murder. State and national leaders need to reconsider our country's priorities and attach more importance to combating violent crime rather than targeting marijuana smokers.

Most Americans do not want to spend public funds incarcerating nonviolent marijuana offenders, at a cost of $23,000 per year.[38] NORML insists that our elected officials recognize that marijuana smokers are not part of the crime problem and it is wasteful, deleterious, and inhumane for our criminal statutes to treat them as if they were.

Marijuana Prohibition Costs Taxpayers at Least $7.5 Billion Annually

While there is a lack of information on the precise costs of marijuana prohibition in the available literature, it is possible to estimate the tremendous annual fiscal costs of marijuana prohibition.

Annual federal government expenditures on the "war on drugs" average $15.7 billion annually.[39] In addition, state and local governments also spend $16 billion per year enforcing drug laws.[40] In 1995, nearly 600,000 of the total 1.5 million drug arrests in America were for marijuana offenses.[41] Therefore, it is reasonable to assume that between 25 and 40 percent of the total $31 billion annual costs are related to marijuana prohibition. Using this basic calculation, marijuana prohibition costs the American taxpayers between $7.5 and $10 billion annually in enforcement alone.

A second way to quantify the costs of marijuana prohibition is to isolate the yearly financial burden inflicted on the criminal justice system by arresting over half a million otherwise law-abiding citizens on marijuana charges. Every time a marijuana arrest occurs — even the most trivial arrest — at least two police officers are taken off the street for several hours to prepare the paperwork and process the defendant. (This occurs even if the individual is allowed to later go free on bond.) If one assumes for simplicity that all the approximately 600,000 marijuana arrests reported in 1995 were simple cases involving no prior use of police time or resources and taking no more than two hours to process, then marijuana prohibition costs law enforcement a minimum of 2,400,000 man hours annually. These are police man hours and fiscal costs that could be better spent targeting violent crime. For example, following the adoption of marijuana decriminalization in California in 1976, the state saved an average of $95.8 million annually.[42]

Of course, these fiscal costs do not end with an arrest. In many instances, police continue to investigate the facts of the case, prosecutors prepare the case for trial or negotiate a plea bargain (estimated at between five and ten hours per case),[43] and judges and court personnel engage in a trial or accept a plea agreement in open court. These prosecutorial costs alone likely cost Americans hundreds of millions of dollars annually.

Clearly more sophisticated economic analysis is needed in this area. Unfortunately, there is no evidence that government is interested in calculating the precise cost of marijuana prohibition because it does not want to have to justify these costs to the American public. It is wasteful and disadvantageous to spend billions of otherwise limited federal dollars on a failed and ineffective public policy at the expense of already underfunded social programs.

Marijuana Prohibition Makes No Exception for Medical Users

Marijuana prohibition applies to everyone, including the sick and dying. Of all the negative consequences of marijuana prohibition, none is as tragic as the denial of medicinal marijuana to the tens of thousands of seriously ill patients who could benefit from its therapeutic use.

It is clear from available studies and rapidly accumulating anecdotal evidence that marijuana is therapeutic in the treatment of a number of serious ailments and is less toxic and costly than the conventional medicines for which it may be substituted. In many cases, marijuana is more effective than the commercially available drugs it replaces. Prestigious groups such as the American Public Health Association, the Federation of American Scientists, and the British Medical Association, as well as *New England Journal of Medicine* editor Jerome Kassirer, publicly endorse the medicinal use of marijuana. Moreover, in 1988, the Drug Enforcement Administration's own chief administrative law judge, Francis L. Young, declared that marijuana was "one of the safest therapeutically active substances known to man."[44]

The best-established medical use of smoked marijuana is as an anti-nauseant for cancer chemotherapy. During the 1980s, smoked marijuana was shown to be an effective anti-emetic in six different state-sponsored clinical studies involving nearly 1,000 patients.[45]

For the majority of these patients, smoked marijuana proved more effective than both conventional prescription anti-nauseants and oral THC (marketed today as the synthetic pill, Marinol). Currently, many oncologists are recommending marijuana to their patients despite its prohibition.[46]

In addition to its usefulness as an anti-emetic, scientific and anecdotal evidence suggests that marijuana is a valuable aid in reducing pain and suffering for patients with a variety of other serious ailments. For example, marijuana alleviates the nausea, vomiting, and the loss of appetite experienced by many AIDS patients without accelerating the rate at which HIV positive individuals develop clinical AIDS or other illnesses.[47] In addition, it is generally accepted — by the National Academy of Sciences (NAS) and others — that marijuana reduces intraocular pressure (IOP) in patients suffering from glaucoma, the leading cause of blindness in the United States.

Clinical and anecdotal evidence also points to the effectiveness of marijuana as a therapeutic agent in the treatment of a variety of spastic conditions such as multiple sclerosis, paraplegia, epilepsy, and quadriplegia. A number of animal studies and a handful of carefully controlled human studies have supported marijuana's ability to suppress convulsions. A summary of these findings was published by the National Academy of Sciences' (NAS) Institute of Medicine in 1982.[48]

Between 1978 and 1996, legislatures in 34 states passed laws recognizing marijuana's therapeutic value. Twenty-five of these laws remain in effect today. Most recently, voters in two states — Arizona and California — overwhelmingly passed laws allowing for the legal use of marijuana under a physician's supervision. Unfortunately, all of these laws are limited in their ability to protect patients from criminal prosecution or provide medical marijuana to those who need it by federal prohibition. In addition, federal officials have threatened to sanction physicians who recommend or use marijuana in compliance with state laws. Clearly, patients who could benefit from marijuana's therapeutic value are being held hostage by a federal government that continues to treat the issue as if it were part of the "war on drugs" instead of a legitimate public health issue. Congress must act to correct this injustice.

When compassion and justice are in conflict with current law, then the law must change.

At NORML's urging, Rep. Barney Frank (D-Mass.), along with co-sponsors Nancy Pelosi (D-Calif.) and Zoe Lofgren (D-Calif.), introduced legislation in Congress on June 4, 1997, that would remove federal obstacles which currently interfere with an individual state's decision to permit the medicinal use of marijuana. H.R. 1782, the "Medical Use of Marijuana Act," allows physicians to legally recommend or prescribe marijuana to seriously ill patients where state law allows them to do so. In addition, it permits states to legally implement different systems of growing and distributing medical marijuana under state law.

H.R. 1782 is not a mandate from Washington and would not require any state to change its current laws. It is a states' rights bill that acknowledges the will of the American people and would allow states to determine for themselves whether marijuana should be legal for medicinal use. It is a common-sense solution to a complex issue and would provide a great deal of relief from suffering for a large number of people. NORML implores Congress to support this compassionate proposal to protect the ten of thousands of Americans who currently use marijuana as a medicine and the millions who would benefit from its legal access. Many seriously ill patients find marijuana the most effective way to relieve their pain and suffering and federal marijuana prohibition must not, in good conscience, continue to deny them that medication.

It Is Time To End Marijuana Prohibition and To Stop Arresting Otherwise Law-Abiding Marijuana Smokers

The "war on drugs" is not really about drugs; if it were, tobacco and alcohol would be the primary targets. They are the most commonly used and abused drugs in America and unquestionably cause far more harm to the user and to society than does marijuana. Yet neither is illegal.

America tried to prohibit alcohol, but soon discovered that the crime and violence associated with prohibition was more damaging than the evil sought to be prohibited. With tobacco, America has learned over the past two decades that education is the most effective way to discourage use. Americans smoke far fewer cigarettes today than in the past without having the criminal justice system issue a single arrest, administer one drug test, seize any property, or sentence anyone to jail. Yet, the federal government fails to apply these lessons toward a rational and effective marijuana policy. Instead, politicians continue to support and enforce a failed, 60-year-old public policy at the expense of rational discourse, billions in misappropriated funds and resources, and many of the founding principles and freedoms that America was built upon. The "war on drugs" has become largely a war on marijuana smokers, and the casualties of this war are the wrecked lives and the destroyed families of the half a million otherwise law-abiding citizens who are arrested each year on marijuana charges.

As a nation we have talked too long in the language of war. It is time to seek a policy that distinguishes between use and abuse, and reflects the importance America places on the right of the individual to be free from the overreaching power of government. Most would agree that the government has no business knowing what books we read, the subject of our telephone conversations, or how we conduct ourselves in the bedroom.

Similarly, whether one smokes marijuana or drinks alcohol to relax is simply not an appropriate area of concern for the government. By stubbornly defining all marijuana smoking as criminal, including that which involves adults smoking in the privacy of their home, government is wasting police and prosecutorial resources, clogging courts, filling costly and scarce jail

and prison space, and needlessly wrecking the lives and careers of genuinely good citizens.

Responsible marijuana smokers present no threat or danger to America, and there is no reason to treat them as criminals. To do so is to wage war without cause against a significant segment of our nation's adult population.

Speaking before Congress on the 40th anniversary of marijuana prohibition — August 2, 1977 — President Jimmy Carter stated: "Penalties against drug use should not be more damaging to an individual than use of the drug itself. Nowhere is this more clear than in the laws against possession of marijuana in private for personal use." Twenty years later, the former president's words ring as urgent as ever. After 60 years of a failed and destructive policy, it is time once and for all to end marijuana prohibition.

Addendum: The Principles of Responsible Use

At NORML, we believe that marijuana smokers, like those who drink alcohol, have a responsibility to behave appropriately and to assure that their recreational drug use is conducted in a responsible manner. Neither marijuana smoking nor alcohol consumption is ever an excuse for misconduct of any kind, and both smokers and drinkers must be held to the same standard as all Americans.

The NORML Board of Directors recently issued the following statement entitled "Principles of Responsible Marijuana Use," which defines the conduct which we believe any responsible adult marijuana smoker should follow.

ADULTS ONLY: Marijuana consumption is for adults

133

only. It is irresponsible to provide cannabis to children. Many things and activities are suitable for young people, but others absolutely are not. Children do not drive cars, enter into contracts, or marry, and they must not use drugs. As it is unrealistic to demand lifetime abstinence from cars, contracts and marriage, however, it is unrealistic to expect lifetime abstinence from all intoxicants, including alcohol. Rather, our expectation and hope for young people is that they grow up to be responsible adults. Our obligation to them is to demonstrate what that means.

NO DRIVING: The responsible marijuana consumer does not operate a motor vehicle or other dangerous machinery impaired by marijuana, nor impaired by any other substance or condition, including some medicines and fatigue. Although marijuana is said by most experts to be safer than alcohol and many prescription drugs with motorists, responsible marijuana consumers never operate motor vehicles in an impaired condition. Public safety demands not only that impaired drivers be taken off the road, but that objective measures of impairment be developed and used, rather than chemical testing.

SET AND SETTING: The responsible marijuana user will carefully consider his/her set and setting, regulating use accordingly. "Set" refers to the consumer's values, attitudes, experience and personality, and "setting" means the consumer's physical and social circumstances. The responsible cannabis consumer will be vigilant as to conditions — time, place, mood, etc. — and does not hesitate to say "no" when those conditions are not conducive to a safe, pleasant and/or productive experience.

RESIST ABUSE: Use of marijuana, to the extent that it impairs health, personal development or achievement, is abuse, to be resisted by responsible cannabis users. Abuse means harm. Some marijuana use is harmful; most is not. That which is harmful should be discouraged; that which is not need not be. Wars have been waged in the name of eradicating "drug abuse," but instead of focusing on abuse, enforcement measures have been diluted by targeting all drug use, whether abusive or not. If marijuana abuse is to be targeted, it is essential that clear standards be developed to identify it.

RESPECT RIGHTS OF OTHERS: The responsible marijuana user does not violate the rights of others, observes accepted standards of courtesy and public propriety, and respects the preferences of those who wish to avoid marijuana entirely. No one may violate the rights of others, and no substance use excuses any such violation. Regardless of the legal status of marijuana, responsible users will adhere to tobacco smoking protocols in public and private places.

References for NORML report

1. Lester Grinspoon, M.D., *Marihuana Reconsidered* (second edition) (San Francisco: Quick American Archives, 1994), p. 11.
2. Grinspoon, p. 11; 'The Hemp Industry in the United States' in *USDA Yearbook* (Washington, DC: U.S. Government Printing Office, 1901), pp. 541-2.
3. Grinspoon, p. 12; John Roulac, *Industrial Hemp: Practical Products — Paper to Fabric to Cosmetics* (Ojai, California: Hemptech Publishing, 1995), p. 8; Rowan Robinson, *The Great Book of Hemp* (Rochester, Vermont: Park Street Press, 1996) pp. 129-133.
4. Wayne D. Rasmussen, ed., *Readings in the History of American Agriculture* (Urbana, Illinois: University of Illinois Press, 1969), p. 296; Roulac, p. 7
5. Grinspoon, p. 17.
6. Robinson, p. 147.
7. U.S. Congress, House, Ways and Means Committee, *Taxation of Marihuana, Hearings on H.R. 6385*, 75th Cong., 1st sess., April 27, 1937, statement of Clinton Hester.
8. Richard J. Bonnie, *The History of the Non-Medical Use of Drugs in the United States: A Speech to the California Judges Association 1995 Annual Conference*, (reprinted not for profit by Iowa NORML, 1997).
9. U.S. Congress, House, Ways and Means Committee, *Taxation of Marihuana, Hearings on H.R. 6385*, statements of Harry Anslinger and Clinton Hester.
10. U.S. Congress, House, Ways and Means Committee, *Taxation of Marihuana, Hearings on H.R. 6385*, statements of William C. Woodward and Rep. Robert L. Doughton.
11. U.S. Congress, House of Representatives, Congressional Record, 75th Cong., 1st sess., June 14, 1937, p. 5575.
12. Substance Abuse and Mental Health Services Administration Office of Applied Studies, *Preliminary Estimates from the 1995 National Household Survey on Drug Abuse* (Washington, DC: U.S. Department of Health and Human Services, 1996), pp. 56-60.
13. Ibid.
14. Ibid.
15. American Civil Liberties Union, *National Surevy of Voters' Opinions on the Use and Legalization of Marijuana for Medical Purposes* (Washington, DC: March 31, 1995 - April 5, 1995).
16. National Commission on Marihuana and Drug Abuse, *Marihuana: A Signal of Misunderstanding*, (Washington, DC: U.S. Government Printing Office, 1972).
17. Federal Bureau of Investigation Uniform Crime Reports, *Crime in the United States: 1972* (Washington, DC: U.S. Government Printing Office, 1973).
18. National Research Council, *An Analysis on Marijuana Policy* (Washington, DC: National Academy Press, 1982).
19. Federal Bureau of Investigation Uniform Crime Reports, *Crime in the United States: 1982* Washington, DC: U.S. Government Printing Office, 1983).
20. Stephen Sidney, M.D. et al., "Marijuana Use and Mortality," *American Journal of Public Health*, April 1997, p. 5.
21. Federal Bureau of Investigation Uniform Crime Reports, *Crime in the United States: 1995* (Washington, DC: U.S. Government Printing Office, 1996).
22. Federal Bureau of Investigation Uniform Crime Reports, *Crime in the United States* (Washington, DC: U.S. Government Printing Office, 1992-1996).
23. National Organization for the Reform of Marijuana Laws, *Citizens' Guide to Marijuana Laws* (Washington, DC: NORML Reports, 1994).
24. Ibid.
25. John Morgan, M.D. and Lynn

Zimmer, Ph.D., *Marijuana Myths, Marijuana Facts: A Review of the Scientific Evidence* (New York City: Lindesmith Center, 1997).

26. Adam Smith, "Pot of Trouble," *Reason Magazine*, May 1997, pp. 47-48.

27. Morgan and Zimmer, *Marijuana Myths, Marijuana Facts: A Review of the Scientific Evidence.*

28. J. Treaster, "Miami Beach's New Drug Weapon: Will Fire Off Letters to the Employer," *New York Times*, February 23, 1991, p. 9.

29. "Thou Hath No Shame: The Czuprynski Affair," *The Champion*, September/October 1995, pp. 27-29.

30. Daryl Kelley, "Investigation of Deputy Urged in Fatal Drug Raid," *Los Angeles Times*, March 31, 1993, p. B4.

31. Morgan and Zimmer, *Marijuana Myths, Marijuana Facts: A Review of the Scientific Evidence.*

32. Ibid.

33. Ibid.; Illinois Department of Corrections, personal communications with Drs. Morgan and Zimmer, October, 1, 1996.

34. Ibid.; California Deptartment of Justice, *Crime and Delinquency in California, 1994* (Sacramento, 1995).

35. Ibid.; New York State Division of Criminal Justice Services, *Characteristics of 1995 Adult Arrestees for Marijuana* (New York City, 1996).

36. Maria L. La Ganga, "DEA Agents Raid Marijuana Club," *Los Angeles Times*, April 22, 1997, p. A3.

37. United States Sentencing Commission, *1994 Annual Report* (Washington, DC: U.S. Sentencing Commission, 1995.), p. 54.

38. Steven R. Donziger, ed., *The Real War on Crime: The Report of the National Criminal Justice Commission* (New York City: HarperPerennial, 1996).

39. Office of National Drug Control Policy, *National Drug Control Strategy, 1997* Washington, DC: ONDCP, 1997).

40. Office of National Drug Control Policy, *State and Local Spending on Drug Control Activities, Report from the National Survey on State and Local Governments* (Washington, DC: ONDCP, 1993)

41. Federal Bureau of Investigation Uniform Crime Reports, *Crime in the United States: 1995* (Washington, DC: U.S. Government Printing Office, 1996).

42. Michael Aldridge and Todd Mikuriqy, M.D., "Savings in California Marijuana Law Enforcement Costs Attributable to the Moscone Act of 1976 — A Summary," *Journal of Psychoactive Drugs*, January/March, 1988.

43. Ibid.

44. *In the Matter of Marihuana Rescheduling Petition, Docket 86-22, Opinion, Recommended Ruling, Findings of fact, Conclusions of Law, and Decision of Administrative Law Judge, September 6, 1988* (Washington, DC: Drug Enforcement Administration, 1988).

45. R.C. Randall, *Cancer Treatment & Marijuana Therapy* (Washington, DC: Galen Press, 1990), pp. 217-243; Kevin Zeese, *Marijuana: Medical Effectiveness Is Proven By Research* (Falls Church, Virginia: Common Sense for Drug Policy, 1997.)

46. Rick Doblin, et al., "Marihuana as Anti-emetic Medicine: A Survey of Oncologists' Attitudes and Experiences," *Journal of Clinical Oncology*: July 1991, pp. 1275-80.

47. Lester Grinspoon, M.D. Et al., *Marihuana, The Forbidden Medicine* (second edition) (New Haven, Connecticut: Yale University Press, 1997); Richard Kaslow, M.D., et al., "No Evidence for a Role of Alcohol or Other Psychoactive Drugs in Accelerating Immunodeficiency in HIV-1 Positive Individuals," *Journal of The American Medical Association*, June 16, 1989, pp. 3424-29.

48. National Academy of Sciences Institute of Medicine, *Marijuana and Health* (Washington, DC: National Academy Press, 1982.)

"sing about a reefer five feet long":

MARIJUANA IN POPULAR MUSIC

by John P. Morgan, M.D.

Introduction

Popular music lyrics and themes focus so often on romantic love that other themes are neglected (money, family, lust, shoes, drugs etc.). For more than 75 years, popular musicians have written, performed, recorded and marketed songs about marijuana. Marijuana apparently goes with all music, for there are examples of "reefer songs" in jazz, Broadway and movie musicals, rock, blues, reggae (and ska), country and western, and hip-hop. Even "The Marijuana Polka" was recorded in 1996.

Marijuana was introduced into the United States by Mexican laborers and the first laws against possession and use of the drug were generated by Texas municipal governments. In *Grass*, this is noted and the story has an early musical accompaniment in "La Cucaracha". This frequently performed and recorded Mexican song, which predates American recorded music, notes that the cockroach does not wish to walk further because he has no marijuana to smoke ("Marijuana te fumar").

Jazz and Reefer

The introduction of marijuana into New Orleans by West Indian seamen was almost contemporaneous with its appearance in Texas. Among early New Orleans users of marijuana were the jazz musicians of the 1920's. Many believe that the spread of marijuana use to the Northern United States was effected to some degree by New Orleans musicians who took the drug with them to St. Louis, Chicago, Kansas City, and New York.

The earliest jazz recordings signifying marijuana's status were instrumentals and the marijuana message was imbedded in the title. Both "The Golden Leaf Strut" (The New Orleans Rhythm Kings) and the "Golden Leaf Rag" (Wingy Mannone) were recorded by New Orleans artists in 1925, the first recorded in New Orleans; the second in Chicago. Louis Armstrong recorded "Muggles" (a New Orleans term for a marijuana cigarette) in 1929.

Marijuana songs early in the next decade were also instrumentals with interpretable titles (a viper is a dedicated user): "The Viper's Drag" (Fats Waller), "The Viper's Moan" ("Mezz" Mezzrow), "Chant of the Weed" (Don Redman), "Blue Reefer Blues" (Richard Jones), and "All Muggled Up" (artist unknown). Obviously, the designation of all the above as marijuana songs relies upon decoding slang and colloquial terms for the drug and its devotees. The employment of language chosen to be understood only by insiders was common when making reference to an illicit pursuit. This use of slang and euphemism characterizes the entire body of marijuana song of all styles. At times, concealment may have been practically important. RCA Victor was reportedly miffed and withdrew promotional support when they learned the actual meaning of Armstrong's "Song of the Vipers" (1935). Most often, however, it seems that the use of slang was really a part of compositional cleverness and not part of an important need to conceal.

Verbal jazz recordings from 1932 to 1945 were incredibly rich in the use of slang and indirect reference. Marijuana was called "tea," "Texas tea," "gage," "stuff," "jive," "mootah" and "reefer." Users were "vipers" and were described as tall, mellow, and high.

The performance style is almost always up-tempo — "let's get high and happy." Marijuana was not viewed as something to promote relaxation. Indeed, its stimulating properties were sought. This phenomenon was grotesquely distorted in film clips seen in *Grass* taken from *Reefer Madness* (originally released as *Teach the Children* in 1937). Piano players begin to pound the keys insanely after a few puffs. In the highs portrayed in recorded jazz music, giddiness or confusion might ensue but all smokers were in control and all had a good time. In "Reefer Man," Cab Calloway sings:

> If he trades you dimes for nickles,
> and calls watermelons pickles,
> then you know you're talkin'
> to the reefer man.

Many of the lyrics used in jazz song actually described the party.

> Close the windows and lock the door.
> Start the party goin' up some more
> Hey, hey, let's all get gay.
> The stuff is here. (Georgia White, 1937)

Andy Kirk and His 12 Clouds of Joy sang that
> The latest craze, the country's rage
> is jive, jive, jive.
> This modern treat makes life complete,
> jive, jive, jive.
> All the jive is gone, all the jive is gone.
> I'm sorry gate, you got here late.
> All the jive is gone. (1936)

"If You're a Viper" was recorded at least four times in the 1930's. "Stuff" Smith's version (sung by Jonah Jones) opened:

> Dream about a reefer five feet long,
> The mighty mezz, but not too strong
> You'll get high but not for long
> If you'se a viper.

Later versions confusingly substituted "a might immense" for "the mighty mezz." A mezz or mezzaroll identified high quality marijuana sold by the clarinetist, Milton Mezzrow. In his 1946 book *(Really the Blues)*, Mezzrow described himself as Harlem's first white marijuana dealer. He also described his first puff of marijuana given by Leon Rappolla, the clarinetist for the New Orleans Rhythm Kings.

In 1937, the year of the marijuana tax act, Cee Pee Johnson described a sad party at Joe's the other night:

> Cats can't buy their jive at night
> So now they hurry home.
> Since the G man got the T man and gone.
> They have to drink their lush and stagger
> Even though they know it's wrong.
> Since the G man got the T man and gone.

The requirement when jive was not available to use other more dangerous drugs, alcohol and others, is a repeated theme in marijuana song.

After the Federal Marihuana Tax Act, Harry Anslinger was more than willing to investigate jazz musicians for federal marijuana-related crimes. It is not known whether the Federal police helped to ensnare Gene Krupa, who was actually subject to a state prosecution in 1943. We assume that Krupa's recording of "I'm Feelin' High and Happy," did not help in his defense.

The end of the jazz era of marijuana music can be dated to the 1945 recording of "Sweet Marijuana Brown."

This slow, laconic piece constituted a warning song:

> Boy, that gal means trouble
> You ought to put her down
> Get hep, take care, look out, beware
> Of Sweet Marijuana Brown.

Tin-Pan Alley

There were two notable show tunes recorded in the 1930's. "Smokin' Reefers" was written by Harold Dietz for a 1934 Broadway show, *Flying Colors*. The singer tells us that

> It's the stuff that dreams are made of,
> It's the stuff that white folks are afraid of
> Up in Harlem, we go on a marijuana jag...
> Smokin' reefers, to get beyond our miseries.

The 1934 movie musical *Murder at the Vanities*, contains a lavishly costumed performance of "Sweet Marihuana," by Gertrude Michel. The song has a Latin staging and appeals to the drug for a narcotic effect to bring home a lost lover, if only in fantasy. The title of "Sweet Marihuana" was later changed to "Lotus Blossom." As such, it was frequently recorded (Julia Lee, Jimmy Witherspoon, Johnny Ray). Bette Midler restored its original title in a 1971 recording.

The Blues

In 1938, Jazz Gillum recorded "Reefer-Headed Woman," a traditional 12-bar blues song. It is also clearly a lamentation about a woman loving reefer too much. The song is not anti-marijuana but does complain about adverse outcomes.

> I can't see why my baby sleeps so sound.
> She musta smoked a reefer.
> It's bound to carry her down.

"Reefer-Headed Woman" is typical of a body of modern blues music in which a male singer laments the consumatory choices of his woman. Champion Jack Dupree sings a "Weed-Headed Woman." Little Mack Simmons, a modern Chicago singer and Aerosmith both have recorded (different) versions of "Reefer-Headed Woman" and Billy-Boy Arnold sings in "Whiskey, Beer, and Reefer" that he doesn't want a woman who stays high all the time. Whiskey-Headed Woman (Lightning Hopkins), "Beer-Headed Woman" (artist unknown) and even a "Jake-Headed Woman"(Black Ace) fill out this list.

Rock and Rock'n'Roll and Reefer

In 1931, the Meltone Boys recorded "Mary Jane," written by Razaf and Robinson who also wrote "Reefer Man":

> Take her to dance,
> Take her to tea.
> It's stunning how cunning
> This girlie can be.
> Gosh, this girl's ideal
> How can she be real?

The lyrics may refer only to a clever girl, but we suspect this song to be the first of many in which marijuana is personified as Mary. This construction became very important in the rock era (post 1964). In "Along Comes Mary," the Association (1965) sings:

> Along comes Mary, and does she wanna
> give me kicks and be my steady chick...

The apposition of Mary and "wanna" was also used by the Dramatics ("Mary Don'tcha Wanna") in 1972. Rick James in "Mary Jane" describes a promiscuous girl "who likes to spread her love around." "Sweet Mary," a 1970 hit for Wadsworth Mansion, is used in *Grass* and therefore becomes a reefer song, although there is nothing in the lyric that makes it so.

The early years of rock generated many songs in which the artist happily used marijuana as imagery, theme, or giggle. "Bass Strings" by Country Joe and the Fish (1967) asked a partner to "pass that reefer 'round." Arlo Guthrie (1969) while "Coming Into Los Angeles," and bringing in a couple of keys, asked the customs man to not touch his bag ("if you please"). Four other songs of this time are used in *Grass*. "Itchycoo Park" (The Small Faces, 1970): "What will we do there? We'll get high." "Rainy Day Woman #12 & #35" (Bob Dylan, 1966): "Then they'll stone you when you're there all alone, everybody must get stoned." "What About Me?" (Quicksilver Messenger Service, 1970):"I smoke marijuana, but I can't get behind your walls, and most of what I believe is against most of your laws." "You Turn Me On" (Ian Whitcomb, 1965): "Come on baby, you really turn me on."

This time of apparent compositional and performing freedom was brief. A 1967 Beatles song ("A Little Help From My Friends") contains "I get high with a little help from my friends." Vice-President Spiro Agnew in a 1970 speech expressed anger about drug mentions in popular music. He was particularly offended by this song because he had learned that the "friends" were actually various drugs. He called upon commercial American radio broadcasters to take responsibility for playing songs which "glorified drugs."

Agnew's words provoked a chilling directive from the Federal Communications Commission. This vague note warned radio programmers that they had to preview all songs to be played and that they should identify (presumably to avoid) those songs with lyrics glorifying drugs.

There is no solid information about radio station response to the directive, but most writers of the time felt that programmers simply avoided playing songs with any identifiable drug content at all. The composer of "King Heroin," a strident anti-drug "rap" by James Brown, believed that the directive caused Brown's recording to be excluded from air time.

"One Toke Over the Line" (Brewer and Shipley, 1971) made it to #7 on the hit charts. Brewer and Shipley felt that the song faded quickly as programmers learned what a "toke" was. The authors and performers took little comfort from a small royalty fee from a gospel choir for recording the song, which did, after all, refer to both sweet Jesus and sweet Mary.

Phil Ochs' "Outside of A Small Circle of Friends" (1972) agreed that smoking marijuana was fun but made the dopers ignore someone who got 30 years for a drug offense. The political nature of the composition did not influence his record company who, after the song attracted some attention, removed the word "marijuana" in fear of the FCC directive.

Country and Western Music

Mainstream country and western artists rarely sing about marijuana. In "I'm the Only Hell My Mama Ever Raised," Johnny Paycheck (1978) sang: "She told me not to smoke it and I did, and it took me far away." Merle Haggard also mildly criticized marijuana use in "Okie From Muskogee" (1969). Such criticism of marijuana in any musical format is unusual. There are however, a large number of songs in C&W *style* about marijuana. These are often recorded by artists who work in country music style but have an urban — even cosmopolitan — sensibility, because they moved from the country or attended college or hung about with the wrong sort of musicians. For example in "Illegal Smile" (1971), John Prine sings: "You may see me tonight, with an illegal smile. It don't cost very much but it lasts a long while." John Hartford (1976) In "Granny Won't You Smoke Some?" claims that "I used to sit around and sing about booze, now I sing about whatever I use."

We think that post-1965, the predominant White presentation for marijuana songs is a city-billy, country-rock style. Often the songs are performed in a laidback, laconic style. They convey a contemporary impression of a marijuana high using musical performance. This approach to the marijuana high contrasts with the up-tempo, dance-and-be-happy performances of jazz musicians of the 30's and 40's described above. "Don't Bogart Me" contains a long-held hesitation on the word "roll" (as in "roll" me another one) as if the singer has forgotten the next note.

Commander Cody is complaining of being "Down to Seeds and Stems Again Blues," but he is so laconic that no desire for obtaining marijuana (or his old girl back) is obvious.

C&W songs often contain narratives, some simple, some very involved. Barefoot Jerry spies a newspaper photo of a friend with "Funny-Looking Eyes," who is in jail for having them. "Panama Red" personifies the drug and its exploits ("he'll steal your woman and he'll wreck your head"). The "Free Mexican Air Force" fancifully delineates a smuggling operation. Both songs were composed by Peter Rowan, a Boston musician who began his professional career singing with Bill Monroe and the Bluegrass Boys.

Both "Wildwood Weed" and "Copperhead Road"

focus, as did songs of alcohol prohibition, on fooling (or eliminating) the government agent. "Copperhead Road" by Steve Earle is wonderfully composed to tell the story of an illegal family distilling operation, replaced by a returning Vietnam veteran with a marijuana planting.

Reggae Music, Ganja Music
The hemp plant as an agricultural source for fiber was grown in North America for hundreds of years. However, the smoking of cannabis came first to Jamaica, brought by and for Indian laborers and indentured servants in the mid-1850's. The smoking of "herb" has been part of Jamaican society for 150 years.

Reggae music developed in Jamaica, incorporating elements of Jamaican folk music, calypso, American rhythm and blues, and rhythmic speech over recordings (dubbing) pushed through enormously powerful sound systems. Reggae was brought to the world in the early 1970's by the recordings of Bob Marley and the Wailers.

The use of marijuana was probably always important to some Jamaican musicians, but its importance is central in reggae. Many reggae musicians are Rastafari — religionists focused on the African origins of Jamaican life and the person of Emperor Haile Selassie (Ras Tafari). The use of marijuana is sacramental to Rastafarianism.

Language related to marijuana appears everywhere in reggae music. The Hindu words *ganja* and *kali* (often "collie" or "collie weed") are used: For example, "Ganja Smokin" (Baja Jedd,19??), "Ganja Man" (Jr. Wilson), "Collie Weed" (Barrington Levy), and "100 Weight of Collie Weed" (Carlton Livingston). The communally passed pipe is often called a chalice: "Chalice in the Palace" (U. Roy). The imagery of community is illuminated by "Chalice In A Circle" (the

141

Mighty Diamonds). Another term for pipe is *kutchie* or *koutchie*. In 1981, the Mighty Diamonds recorded the song, "Pass The Kutchie." The song became a very big hit for a kid reggae group (Musical Youth). However, it was renamed "Pass the Dutchie"(1982). A "dutchie" in Jamaica is a cooking pot. An early Wailers recording, "Dutch Pot," also referred to a cooking vessel but is occasionally thought to be a marijuana song. So, "Pass the Dutchie" ("from the left hand side"), overtly about a communal meal, is a song about passing a ganja pipe.

Other colloquial terms for ganja are "chronic," "weed," "herb," and "sensi" (from sensemilla, smoking material from an unfertilized potent female plant). A "spliff" is a large cone-shaped cigarette filled with ganja; see "The Chronic" (Beenie Man and Silver Cat), "Jamaican Weed" (Lone Ranger, 1978), "Legalize The Herb" (Ninjaman, 1990), "Under Mi Sensi" (Barrington Levy, 1985), "Macka Spliff" (Steel Pulse), "Sinsemilla" (Black Uhuru, 1980). Bob Marley recorded two ganja songs, "Kaya" and "Easy Skankin".

There are consistent marijuana themes in reggae. One frequently repeated is a preference for ganja over cocaine: ("Weed Not Coke," Baby Wayne; "Don't Sniff Coke," Pato Blanton). Blanton states: "I do not sniff the coke, I only smoke sensemilla."

A political theme opposing criminalization is often developed. John Holt in "Police In Helicopter" warns: "If you continue to burn the herb, we're gonna burn down the cane fields". Peter Tosh's "Legalize It" may be the most familiar ganja anthem of all. Tosh performed "Legalize It" on *Saturday Night Live* in 1978.

One of the most influential American reggae songs (performed by a white California band) is "Smoke Two Joints" (The Toyes, 1991). It has been covered by a heavy-metal band (Sublime), quoted in a video ("Many Clouds of Smoke," Total Devastation, 1993), and is played every day at 4:20 PM by an Oakland radio station.

> *I smoke two joints in the morning,*
> *I smoke two joints at night.*
> *I smoke two joints in the afternoon,*
> *It makes me feel all right.*

Rap and Reefer

Rhymed rhythmic speech in public performance is an American cultural facet which moved in an unbroken line from Africa to the Caribbean to the USA. Rap (or hip-hop) uses rhymed and rhythmic talk in a kind of vernacular poetry, which has been present in America in children's chanting, work songs by the dozens, tobacco auctioneering, oratory, and boasts and toasts. Contemporary rap in America is deeply indebted to the Jamaican phenomenon of dub, deejaying, or emceeing, in which rhythmic rhyming slang is improvised at a dance hall over an existing instrumental soundtrack. Count Machuki, a Jamaican often called the foundation deejay — the first to talk over records — said: "I had to get more things to say... I see a magazine called *Jive*. I took up that magazine and saw something that amused me...And from there on I was able to create my own jives."

Grandmaster Flash said: "Hip-hop is the only genre that allows us to talk about most anything." Since the release of "Rapper's Delight" in 1979, that "most anything" has frequently involved drugs. Almost without exception, rap has railed against cocaine and been very soft on marijuana.

In "Jane, Stop This Crazy Thing", MC Shan (Cold Chillin', 1986) says:

> *Jane got weak, and the base got strong*

What she used to do right, Jane now does wrong.
I walked by one day, called to my man Jack,
She almost broke her neck, cause she thought
I said crack.

Some jazz musicians thought that marijuana use was important as an aid to creativity. Louis Armstrong reportedly encouraged other musicians to smoke, particularly before recording. The belief in marijuana's nourishment of verbal creativity in rappers is strong. In "Spark Mad Izm" (Channel Live, 199?), we hear:

> *Wake in the morning got the yearning for herb,*
> *Which loosens up the nouns, metaphors and*
> *   verbs*
> *And adjectives, ain't it magic kid what I'm*
> *   kicking...*

And Tone Loc says;

> *Go behind tha curtains while my fans they*
> *   point*
> *You know what Loc's doin', I'm blazin' a joint,*
> *Cause it seems a lot of times' I'm at my best*
> *After some methical or a bowl of sense.*
> *I'm creatin', multiplyin, big time supplying'...*
> *("Cheeba, Cheeba", 1990).*

The approval of marijuana use by the rap community is so strong many artists have chosen names to remind us of that commitment. There are Eddie Cheeba, Ganjah K., Canibus, Mean Green, and Spliff Star.

The evolving of a new genre means much new slang. We learned that both "bammer weed" and "stress" are bad marijuana. "Don't Give Me No Bammer Weed"

(RBL Posse, 1992). Marijuana is called "chronic," "cheeba," "sence" or "sense," "blunt," "methical," "ism," "buddah," "skunk," "dank," "indo," or "blunt."

Cypress Hill was identified as the stoner band of the decade at the High Times 25th Anniversary Party. They have recorded "I Wanna Get High," "Legalize It," "Stoned Is The Way of The Walk," and "Dr. Greenthumb." "Hits From The Bong" exclaims:

> *Let's smoke that bowl*
> *hit that bong, and then take that finger off*
> *the hole.*
> *Plug it unplug it, don't strain.*
> *I love you Mary Jane.*

Other reefer'n' rap anthems (mostly self explanatory): "How To Roll A Blunt," (Redman) describes the loading of marijuana into a tobacco cigar, the Philly Blunt; "I Got 5 On It" (The Luniz) describes a contribution for the up-front purchase of a significant amount of contraband; in Tha Alkoholiks version of "Mary Jane," "she's (still) got that kind of love that needs to be spread around"; In "Grow Room," DJ Pooh writes:

> *It's not been three months*
> *I'm tempted to break off a piece and roll*
> *   some blunts*
> *I wonder what it is, is this some skunk?*
> *I see some purple stems and orange hairs*
> *Could it be the Humboldt mixed with Maui?*
> *It's a hybrid*
> *Wow! Look what I did.*

In "Pack the Pipe," Pharcyde extols the use of marijuana to curtail risky pipe use of another kind altogether

143

(a "Sherm" refers to a cigarette from Nat Sherman, a tobacconist on 5th Avenue, dipped in PCP):

> *Why does your mother smoke pipe*
> *with crack on the inside*
> *she likes to take a bus ride with a Sherm stick*
> *in her mouth.*

The one rap song used in the *Grass* soundtrack ("How High," Method Man and Redman) does contain some reefer reference:

> *Look up in the sky, it's a bird it's a plane.*
> *It's the funk doctor Spock smokin' buddah on*
> *a train...*

But the song seems mostly about guns (Glock, Smif'n'Wes, AK matic, and 12 gauge Mossberg) and their uses.

Conclusion

All types of music and musicians employ marijuana images and references. As well as the styles and artists mentioned above, popular music in Brazil occasionally discusses "maconha," and a large volume of music, *rebetica*, made by Greek exiles from Asia Minor, after the establishment of modern Turkey, sings of the use of hashish.

In America, musicians from the earliest days of recorded music to today have played and sung about reefer. They've employed astonishing numbers of slang terms and euphemisms in reference to the drug. They liked to describe people who were high and they loved to describe marijuana parties. They've suggested replacing other drugs with marijuana, and they are often important sources suggesting drug policy reform, decriminalization, and legalization.

White musicians in a self-conscious (and "artistic") manner have used references to marijuana to establish their hipness and outsider credentials. African-American artists in the oldest (jazz) and newest (rap) formats have incorporated reefer references easily and not self-consciously from the culture in which they lived. Much of this culturally consonant music (jazz and rap) is to us compelling, exciting, and skilled. We'll leave it to you the listener to determine whether the use of marijuana makes for better music; our survey shows that using marijuana references may have that effect.

Produced and Directed by	Ron Mann
Narrator	Woody Harrelson
Writer	Solomon Vesta
Sound Design	Rosnick Mackinnon
Original Music Score	Guido Luciani
Graphics Co-Ordinator	Maury Whyte
Art Director	Paul Mavrides
Editor	Robert Kennedy
Co-Producer	Sue Len Quon
Executive Producer	Keith Clarkson
Associate Producer	Marc Glassman
Head Researcher	Rani Singh
Research Consultant	Rick Prelinger
Good Advice	Bill Schroeder
Director Of Photography	Robert Fresco
Executive Sound Design	Ted Rosnick
Sound Design	Mike Rosnick, Tom Trafalski
Re-Recording Mixer	Keith Elliott
Assistant Mixer	Mark Zsifkovits
Assistant Editor	Sue Len Quon
Dialogue Editor	Mishann Lau
Assistant Dialogue Editor	Sean Moriarity
Music Editor	Robert Kennedy
Sound Effects Programming	Tom Trafalski
Foley Artist	Andy Malcolm
Foley Assistant	Sharon Zupancic
Foley Mixer	Ron Mellegers
Sound Transfers	Larry Johnson
Film Research	Lewanne Jones
Researchers	Craig Baines, Michael Boyuk, Michael Dolan, Daniel Garber Marc Glassman, Heather Gray Rosemary Heather, Maria Lindberg Theresa Rowat, David Segal Kika Thorne, Oliver Trager
Historical Consultant	Benedikt Fischer
Statistical Research	Saima Anto
Editorial Consultants	Gerald Peary, Bill Schroeder
Production Supervisor	Sue Len Quon
Assistant To The Producer	Heather Gray
Production Assistants	Peter Heidemann, Richard Mackenzie, Josh Perell, Naomi Powell, Brigette Sachse
Opening Title Design	Paul Mavrides
Opening Title Animation	Vello Virkhaus
Cg Animation/Graphics	Paul Mavrides
Cg Animation Assistant	Dana Smith
Cg Art Assistant	Mimi Heft

Cg Animation Rendering	Bert Monroy
Digital Art Assistants	Phoebe Gloeckner, Bert Monroy
Inferno Artist	Steven Lewis
Digital Effects Post	Spin Productions
Digital Rendering	David Biedny, Idig Inc.
Film Recording	Cine-Byte Imaging Inc.
Stone Age Animation	Maury Whyte
Animation Camera	Bob Mistysyn
Additional Camera	Jermaine Love
Post Production Sound	Deluxe Toronto, Rosnick Mackinnon, Tattersall Sound, Todd-Ao Studios
Dolby Sound Consultant	Eric Christoffersen
Opticals	Film Effects
Additional Opticals	Film Opticals Of Canada
Lab	Deluxe Toronto
Timer	Leslie D'brass
Negative Cutter	Catherine Rankin
Accountant	Glenn Fraser
Bookkeeper	Paul Hillerup
Legal	Gary Solway
Insurance	Aon/Ruben-Winkler
Film Angel	Vic Peters
Additional Dialogue	Saima Anto, Gordan Bryant David Bryant, Ian Busher, James Calero, Bill Carroll, Keith Clarkson, Christopher Dunlop, Jim Dunlop, Mini Holmes, Bob Kobres, Eric Kulberg, George Logogianes, Fred Macdonald, Craig Malcolm, Haley Mann, Richard Maxwell, Maureen S. Morris, David Ossman, Charles Pascal, Eli Perell, Josh Perell, Philip Proctor, Harry S. Robins, Mike Rosnick, Rick Shekter, Harry Shearer, Robert Skates, Earl Sky, Rev. Ivan Stang, Vic Varney, Stephanie Zari
Peerless Adr Casting	Michael Packer
Adr Recording	Tim Fisher, Kevin Schultz, Weldon Brown
Music Consultants	Rob Bowman, Elliott Lefko
Music Clearance	Ann Mayall

Quit Playing Games With God !
Written And Performed By Mark Mothersbaugh
Produced By Mark Mothersbaugh/ Bob Casale
Engineered And Mixed By Bob Casale
Additional Sampling Albert Fox

Recorded At Mutato Muzika West Hollywood
Published By Mutato Muzika Bmi, 1999

All The Jive Is Gone
Performed By Andy Kirk & His Twelve Clouds Of Joy
Is Reproduced By Arrangement With
Universal Music Canada

Barnyard In Orbit
Performed By Jean Jacques Perrey & Gershon Perrey
Courtesy Of Vanguard Records/A Welk Music Group Co.
By Arrangement With Warner Special Products
And Fiedel Music Industries

Bustin' Out
Performed By Rick James
Is Reproduced By Arrangement With
Jobete Music Company And Universal Music Canada

Cocaine
Performed By J.J. Cale
Is Reproduced By Arrangement With
Audigram Songs Inc. And Universal Music Canada

Fresh Air
As Recorded By Quicksilver Messenger Service
Is Reproduced By Arrangement With Mobetta Music
And Emi Music Canada

Hooray For Hollywood
By Arrangement With Harms Inc.

I Get A Kick Out Of You
Performed By Dinah Washington
Is Reproduced By Arrangement With Harms Inc.
And Universal Music Canada

If You're A Viper
Performed By Rosetta Howard
Is Reproduced By Arrangement With
Mca Duchess Music Corporation
And Universal Music Canada

Illegal Smile
Performed By John Prine
Is Reproduced By Arrangement With
Sour Grapes Music/Walden Music
And Oh Boy Records

Itchycoo Park
Performed By Small Faces
Is Reproduced By Arrangement With
Emi Music Publishing Inc./Immediate Music Ltd.
And Charly Records

I Want To Take You Higher
Performed By Sly And The Family Stone
Courtesy Of Warner-Tamerlane Publishing Co.
And Sony Music Entertainment Inc.
By Arrangement With
Sony Music Entertainment (Canada) Inc.

Killin' Jive
By Arrangement With
Mca Duchess Music Corporation

Legalize It
Performed By Peter Tosh
Courtesy Of Irving Music Inc.
And Sony Music Entertainment Inc.

Magnificent Seven Theme
As Recorded By Al Caiola
Is Reproduced By Arrangement With
Emi Music Publishing Inc. And Emi Music Canada
Man With The Golden Arm
As Recorded By Billy May
Is Reproduced By Arrangement With
Dena's Trust And Emi Music Canada

Marahuana
Performed By Gertrude Michael
By Arrangement With Famous Music

Mr. Big Stuff
Performed By Jean Knight
Is Reproduced By Arrangement With
Caraljo Music Inc./Malaco Music Company
And Fantasy Inc.

Okie From Muskogee
As Recorded By Merle Haggard
Is Reproduced By Arrangement With Sony/Atv Songs
And Emi Music Canada

One Toke Over The Line
Performed By Brewer & Shipley
Is Reproduced By Arrangement With
Careers Bmg Music Publishing And Bmg Records

Pammie's On A Bummer
Performed By Sonny Bono
Is Reproduced By Arrangement With
Cotillion Music Inc. And Warner Special Products

Rainy Day Women #12 & 35
Written By Bob Dylan
Performed By A Subtle Plague
Courtesy Of Special Rider Music

Reefer Man
Performed By Cab Calloway
By Arrangement With
Emi Music Publishing Inc./Warner Chappell Music

Satan Is Real
As Recorded By The Louvin Brothers
Is Reproduced By Arrangement With
Emi Music Publishing Inc. And Emi Music Canada

Sendin' The Vipers
By Arrangement With
Denton & Haskins Corporation

South Of The Border
Performed By Brass From Tijuana
Is Reproduced By Arrangement With
Shapiro Bernstein & Co Inc.
And Madacy Music Group

Sweet Leaf
By Arrangement With Essex Music International Inc.

Sweet Mary
Performed By Wadsworth Mansion
Is Reproduced By Arrangement With
Emi Music Publishing Inc.

Takin' It To The Streets
Performed By The Doobie Brothers
Is Reproduced By Arrangement With Tauripin Tunes
And Warner Special Products

Viper Mad
Performed By Sidney Bechet
Is Reproduced By Arrangement With
Mca Duchess Music Corporation
And Universal Music Canada

What Kind Of Fool Am I?
By Arrangement With Ludlow Music Inc.

You Turn Me On
Performed By Ian Whitcomb
Is Reproduced By Arrangement With
Ian Whitcomb Songs And Celebrity Licensing Inc.

Original Score
Produced By Mike Rosnick And Ted Rosnick
Orchestrated And Conducted By Guido Luciani
Recorded And Mixed At Manta/Eastern Sound By John Naslen Assisted
By Annelise Noronha

All Because Of Maureen S. Morris

Soundtrack Available On
Mercury Records

Soundtrack Produced By
Big Picture Entertainment

Soundtrack Executive Producers
Lewis/Stegall/Kates/Florita

Stock Footage Supplied By: Abcnews Videosource, John E. Allen, Archive Films, Inc., Budget Films, Inc., Jimmy Carter Library, Cbs News Archive, Chertock And Associates, The Cinema Guild,Inc., Peter Conheim, F.I.L.M. Archives, Don Haig, The Harvey Group, Hot Shots/Cool Cuts, John F.Kennedy Library Foundation, Library Of Congress, Macdonald And Associates, National Archives And Records Administration, Nixon Presidential Materials Project National Archives, Nbc News Archives, Oddball Film And Video, San Francisco, Original Filmvideo Library, Oregon Historical Society, Producers Library Service, Sherman Grinberg Film Libraries, Inc., Something Weird Video/Shock Stock, Universal Media, Inc., Ucla Film And Television Archive, University Of South Carolina, Louis Wolfson Ii Media History Center

Be-In	Courtesy Of Jerry Abrams
Dragnet	International House
Murder At The Vanities	Held Under Copyright And Licensed From Universal City Studios, Inc
Pursued	Courtesy Of Republic Entertainment Inc.
Saturday Night Live	Courtesy Of Broadway Video Entertainment And Nbc Studios
Smoke-In	Courtesy Of Dana Beal
Ten For Two	Courtesy Of Yoko Ono Print Courtesy Of Steve Gebhardt
United Nations	Courtesy Of United Nations Department Of Public Information
	By Providing Footage The United Nations Does Not Necessarily Share The Views Contained In The Production.
Up In Smoke	Courtesy Of Paramount Pictures Corp.
Woodstock	Courtesy Of Warner Bros.
Wsb Television Newsfilm	Provided By The Wsb Television Newsfilm Collection University Of Georgia Libraries Media Archives

Photos Courtesy Of : Ap/ Wide World Photos, Archive Photos, Bentley Historical Library, University Of Michigan, Corbis Historical Collections And Labor Archives, Penn State, Library Of Congress, Louis Armstrong House And Archives, Queens College/Cuny National Archives And Records Administration, Harry S. Truman Library, United Nations Department Of Public Information

Articles Courtesy Of: Academy Of Motion Picture Arts And Sciences, Historical Collections And Labor Archives, Penn State National Archives And Records Administration

Newsweek   Courtesy Of Newsweek Magazine

Marihuana A Signal
Of Misunderstanding   Courtesy Of Penguin Putnam Inc.

The Freak Brothers Pull A Heist
Published By Rip Off Press, Inc.
In The Collected Adventures Of
The Fabulous Furry Freak Brothers (Tm)
Copyright (C) 1970 And 1997 By Gilbert Shelton
All Rights Reserved

Cost Of The U.S. War On Marijuana
Prepared By Barbara Herring & Associates
Numbers Represent An Average Cost Per Year In 1998 Dollars.

Statistics Sourced From
Fbi Uniform Crime Reports 1976-1998
Shafer Committee 1970
Compendium Of Federal Justice Statistics 1993
Historical Corrections Statistics 1850-1984
Marijuana Arrests And Incarceration In The United States, Marijuana
Policy Project 1998

For More Information See
www.lindesmith.org
www.norml.org

Special Thanks To
Michael Aldrich, John Allen, Adrienne Andrews, Alan Bak, Jeff Baker, Derrick Beckner, Diane Boehme, Tammy Boyling, Peter Conheim, Steve Davidson, Dale R. De La Torre, J.R. "Bob" Dobbs, Jim Fleming, Clara Fon-Sing, Stan Ford, Rob Fulton, George Furniotis, Toni Gavin, Kim Gertler, Joel Goldberg, Candice S. Hanson, Sherie Harding, Brett Harrelson, Tracy Harshman, Howard Hays, Mimi Heft, Jan-Christopher Horak, Michael Horowitz, Barbara Humphries, Eric Kulberg, Annie Lewis, Pam Linton, Fred Macdonald, Harold Mann, Madeline Matz, Susan Mcglashan, Kate Mckay, Joe Medjuck, Robin Mirsky, Patrick Montgomery, Charles Moore, Ethan A. Nadelmann, Scott Norman, Harold Phillips, Nick Pitt, Josh Raphaelson, Jan Rofekamp, Jonathan Rosenbaum, Chris Ross, Jeff Sackman, Gerlinde Scharinger, Screen Actors Guild, Alexa-Francis Shaw, Jim Shedden, William Shurk, Ann Sperling, Michael Starks, Bob Stein, Patricia Tice, Mark Tusk, Mike Vrainey, Wendy Williams, Peter Lamborn Wilson, S.C. Wilson, World Litho, Mike Zryd,

Jay Switzer
And
Paty, Haley, Sophie, Oliver & Rae

Financing Facilitated By R&R Joint Enterprises Inc.

Produced With Financial Assistance From
The Cable Production Fund
The Ontario Film Investment Program
Rogers Telefund

Produced In Association With
Chumcity

Dolby Digital In Selected Theaters

No Hippies Were Harmed In The Making Of This Movie.

This Motion Picture Is Protected
Under International And Pan-American
Copyright Conventions. No Part Of This
Film May Be Reproduced Or Transmitted
In Any Form Or By Any Means
Without Written Permission.

Sphinx Productions
Copyright MCMXCIX

ron mann

Ron's alternative brand of documentary films has made him a festival and critics' favorite, except maybe in his home province of Ontario, Canada, where "Grass" was banned by the Ontario Review Board. Ron is currently at work on a new movie with actor/activist Woody Harrelson about "the need for people to wrench themselves from the corporate grid."